NOT TO WORRY, MOM,
I'M OKAY

Lessons in Living from a Beloved Son

NOT TO WORRY, MOM, I'M OKAY

Lessons in Living from a Beloved Son

Karma Smith Belnap

Covenant Communications, Inc.

Published by Covenant Communications, Inc.
American Fork, Utah

Printed in the United States of America
First Printing: March 1996

01 00 99 98 97 96   10 9 8 7 6 5 4 3 2 1

ISBN 1-55503-931-6

In memory of
Lee Smith Belnap

Dedicated with love to my husband, Kay,
and our children: Mary, Patricia, Irene,
Stanley, Steven, and Roger

I regret that space limitations have not allowed me to more than touch on the lives of my other six children and my husband, Kay. My children have always been, and continue to be, a source of great joy to me; and Kay has been the rock from which I've gained strength and wisdom these past fifty years.

* * * * * *

This work is written from my personal perspective as Lee's mother and is based on my journal entries and recollection of events that occurred between 1963 and 1991. It is also based on Lee's journal, letters, tapes, and medical records. To improve readability, time sequences have occasionally been altered and literary license taken in the retelling of minor incidents.

Introduction

It takes courage to live—courage and strength and hope and humor. And courage and strength and hope and humor have to be bought and paid for with pain and work and prayers and tears.

—Jerome P. Fleishman

Our son, Lee, lived his twenty-eight years with courage, strength, hope, and humor. And, yes, often that courage, strength, hope, and humor was paid for with pain and work and prayers and tears.

Initially, this book was intended to be solely about Lee. But as a family, our lives were so intertwined that its scope became much broader. The book, therefore, is also the story of our family—how we responded to Lee's challenges, and how his life affected ours. As his mother, I have been particularly affected and moved by his extraordinary response to the difficult circumstances of his life.

Lee was born with cystic fibrosis. He knew at an early age that ultimately the disease would destroy his body, but he was determined that it would never conquer his spirit—the "Lee" part of him, as he called it. In this, he succeeded admirably; and in the process, he unknowingly taught his family many unforgettable lessons.

Lee's trust in the Lord gave him the inner strength and resilience to bounce back time after time when faced with adversity and disappointment. His faith, zest for life, and "never give up" attitude inspired, and continue to inspire, his family and friends. In sharing his story, my prayer is that readers will also be inspired and uplifted, especially during those troubled times that beset all of us in this beautiful, but imperfect world.

Karma Smith Belnap

Prologue

I wanted to cry and scream and rage, anything to release the crushing pain that had been building inside me for days and weeks and years. But instead I sat silently beside my daughter, Irene, waiting for the plane that was bringing my youngest son home for the last time. The wheelchair and oxygen tank we had picked up earlier that day stood nearby, mute evidence of his deteriorating condition.

I knew Irene was suffering, too, and I longed to take her in my arms and comfort her, but I didn't dare. We mustn't be crying when they wheeled Lee off the plane. He wouldn't want that.

For twenty-eight years, Lee had waged a defiant battle against cystic fibrosis, and now it was nearly over. He was coming home to die.

Oh, he hadn't worded it that way when he'd phoned from the University of Washington Medical Center in Seattle a few days before. That wasn't his style. He had simply said, "It's time for me to come home."

"Time to come home." Nearly two years had passed since the day he had told his father and me that he didn't want to die in a hospital. When his time came, he wanted to die at home in his own room. He would know when to come home. Now he was coming.

Beginnings

Many years have passed since Lee was born on May 10, 1963. But I remember well the first time I held him in my arms and looked into that tiny face with its perfect features. How fresh from God he was! Enchanted, I pushed the baby-fine, blond hair into a little curl on top of his head and traced the graceful arch of his dark brows with my fingertips. At my touch he uncurled his clenched fist, and I placed my finger in his wrinkled palm. His fingers, surprisingly strong, closed around it.

Squirming against the confining receiving blanket, he opened birth-swollen eyes and squinted past me. I crooned his name, and his eyes wandered around until they fastened on mine. An indescribable love for this new little son surged through me, and I felt my spirit bond with his in a mother-son relationship that I knew would endure forever.

Lee joined a large and lively family. Mary, at fourteen, was already budding into an attractive young lady and was heavily involved in piano, 4-H, and school and church activities. As our firstborn, she was a willing "second mother" to her younger sisters and brothers.

Patty, twelve, was a quiet, private girl who preferred practicing her flute or curling up in a quiet corner with a book to engaging in the often boisterous activities of her siblings. On the other hand, Irene, eleven, didn't have a quiet bone in her body. Always on the move and always ready with a tale to tell, her presence brought a room alive. Like her sisters, she participated in many activities; but her greatest love was dancing, and she often performed as an acrobatic dancer.

Stanley, with his deep dimples and engaging grin, was barely eight and a favorite of the little girls at school. He knew this for a fact because they only kicked boys on the shins that they liked, and his were constantly bruised!

Steven, at the tender age of five, was already fine-tuned to the moods and needs of others. He was on the shy side, and he surveyed new situations warily—that is, unless a ball was involved. Then he became a fearless competitor.

Affectionate Roger of the chocolate brown eyes was a warm, cuddly three-year-old who quickly snuggled into any available lap. And there were plenty of those!

I met my husband, Kay, at the University of Idaho when I was a senior. He had just returned from serving three combat tours in the South Pacific as a Marine dive bomber pilot, and was finishing his studies at the university. If it wasn't love at first sight, it was close, and we married a few months later.

After graduating, we moved to Boise, Idaho. In 1963, when Lee was born, Kay was spending his days as Chief of Administration of the Idaho Fish and Game Department and his evenings and weekends doing those things that bishops in The Church of Jesus Christ of Latter-day Saints do.

Lee was six weeks old when he showed the first symptoms of cystic fibrosis. However, at that time, many physicians were not alert to the symptoms of the disease, and our family doctor and neighbor, Dr. Bernard P. Strouth, diagnosed his problem as a milk allergy. We put him on a soybean formula.

At first, the new formula seemed to be working; but then came the morning when we almost lost him. I was making sandwiches at the kitchen counter when Stanley, who was sitting beside me rocking him, screamed, "He's choking!"

I whirled to see Lee's little back arch, his arms flailing frantically above his head. His face turned a dirty blue. I snatched him from Stan, but even as I did, his struggles ceased and his body sagged in my arms. He appeared lifeless. I tilted his head back and covered his nose and mouth with my mouth. Forcing myself to breathe shallowly, I blew a short breath into his mouth. His chest didn't move.

Again I blew. Nothing! Clearly, the air wasn't reaching his lungs, but I didn't dare blow harder. Was something lodged in his throat? I swung him head down, his body limp against my outstretched legs, and slapped him sharply on the back. Nothing! Fighting hysteria, I clapped his back again and again, all the time praying, "Oh, God, help me. Don't let him die!"

Suddenly, a wad of dark mucus shot out of his mouth. Not wasting a second, I laid him on the floor and pushed on his chest with the flat of my fingers. Push, release, push, release. After what seemed like an eternity, he sucked in a breath, breathed raggedly for a few seconds, and then, filling his lungs with air, began to scream.

Minutes later, I was in Dr. Strouth's office. He checked Lee thoroughly. No temperature, no rattles in his lungs, not even a pink throat. He took a chest x-ray; it, too, was normal.

"I don't think you need to worry about him choking again," the doctor said. "There must have been some mucus in his lungs when he was born, and it gradually worked its way up until it lodged in his throat. He's all right now. But I'm going to switch him to a different formula. He's losing weight, and I don't like that."

Lee didn't choke again, but he continued to lose weight. Dr. Strouth tried formula after formula, but the weight loss continued. Not only that, but now he had several bulky bowel movements a day, and he was wheezing. Something was wrong. But what?

In the middle of July, Elder N. Eldon Tanner spoke at our stake conference as the visiting General Authority. At the request of our stake president, Elder Tanner came to our home between sessions and administered to Lee. In anticipation of the special blessing, we held a family meeting early that morning, and Kay bore testimony to the children of the power of the priesthood in healing the sick. He reminded them of the many times they had received this blessing in their lives. Passing around a picture of Elder Tanner, he explained his calling as a member of the

Quorum of the Twelve Apostles. At the close of our meeting, Irene suggested that we fast until after the blessing, and we agreed this was something we should do.

While Kay and the children attended conference, I stayed home to care for Lee, bathing him and dressing him in the little white knit suit the Relief Society presidency had given me when he was born. It was several sizes too large, but it camouflaged his painfully thin body; and I wanted him to look his very best for Elder Tanner.

Upon his arrival, Elder Tanner shook hands with the children, looked deep into their round, solemn eyes, and called them by name. It was an experience they never forgot, and years later they would tell their own children about the time this great man shook their hand and called them by name. Now, at Elder Tanner's request, Mary gave a brief prayer, and then, assisted by Kay and the stake president, he placed his hands upon Lee's head and gave him a blessing.

All morning I had prayed that Elder Tanner would be impressed to promise Lee a speedy and complete recovery. But it was not to be. Instead, we were assured that the Lord was mindful of him and of our family and that, dependent upon our diligence and faithfulness, He would give us the guidance, courage, and strength to care for this special little spirit who graced our home. This promise was literally fulfilled time after time during Lee's life.

In looking back, I can see the Lord's hand in guiding us a few days later to the doctor who not only recognized the symptoms of cystic fibrosis in a day when this was not generally the case, but who stubbornly stuck by his diagnosis in spite of faulty lab results. His name was William L. Venning, a pediatric allergist.

Carrying a high, three-legged stool, he strode into the examining room. He was tall, somewhat on the slender side, possibly in his late forties, with piercing dark eyes and long black sideburns. Years before, spinal surgery had left him with a permanently stiff back, and the stool he carried was specially designed to save him from bending over the examining table.

Nodding in my general direction, he motioned for me to lay Lee on the padded table; and with a curt, "You have a very ill baby here," he began his examination.

He took x-rays and blood tests. He measured Lee's head and chest and kneaded his distended stomach. He flexed his arms, legs, and neck, and listened to his heart and lungs, pausing only to bark an occasional question at me as he thoroughly explored every inch of the little wasted body. All the while, Lee screamed furiously at this stranger's poking and probing. An eternity later, he motioned for me to pick the baby up.

"We're dealing with something more than an allergy here," he said shortly. "I have an idea what it is, but I need to run a test to be certain. It'll take an hour or so." I asked him what he was looking for, but he only growled, "No use worrying you with what I think it is until we find out for certain. It's something I'm sure you've never heard of; and if he doesn't have it, there's no sense upsetting you."

With those unsettling words, he motioned me to a chair in the corner of the room and left. In a few minutes he was back with his nurse, Dortha. Together they slipped Lee's arm into a thin plastic bag and wrapped it in several towels. He explained that Lee would have to sweat for an hour before they could administer the test.

They left the room. Lee, exhausted from crying, fell asleep in my arms, his long black lashes partially masking the dark hollows beneath his eyes. Sick with apprehension, I sat stiffly in the straight-backed chair, throat dry, heart pounding, terror knotting my insides. Unconsciously, my grip on Lee tightened. His warm little body stiffened in protest, but he didn't awaken. Taking deep breaths to calm myself, I became aware of voices in the adjoining room.

"Hey there, Davey, I hear you've got a cold in your nose, nose, nose, and it's dripping like a hose, hose, hose." A child laughed delightedly, and Dr. Venning joined in with a hearty laugh of his own.

I was surprised. During the brief time we'd spent together, Dr. Venning had been coldly professional, even intimidating. I was relieved by this glimpse of a warmer side.

At last, he and Dortha returned. They freed Lee's arm from its plastic prison and carefully pressed his tiny hand onto a red, gel-like substance in a small dish. When the doctor removed it, a clear, yellowish-white imprint remained. The nurse's quick intake of breath and the almost imperceptible sag of Dr. Venning's shoulders told me without words that the test was positive.

Expressionless, the doctor turned to me and said, "The test was for an extremely serious disease, cystic fibrosis. It's quite rare, and you've probably not heard of it. The screening test I ran isn't as accurate as the more sophisticated ones performed in hospitals, but he has all the symptoms of the disease. We'll test him later in the hospital; but first we have to treat him for pneumonia, probably staph. Results of the culture will tell us for certain."

Before I could speak, he looked at his watch. "Dortha will give him an antibiotic by injection now, but I can't shake free to admit him to the hospital for another couple of hours. You may as well take him home. Just make certain you have him at St. Luke's in two hours."

He turned, but before he could leave, I forced myself to ask, "How bad is he?"

The veiled look in his eyes gave me my answer. He didn't expect Lee to live. However, all he said was, "Pneumonia is extremely serious in a normal baby this young, and when you add the possibility of cystic fibrosis—" He shrugged his shoulders and left the room.

I don't recall walking out of the doctor's office or getting into my car. When I came to myself, a van was passing me in the opposite direction, horn blaring, its teenaged occupants gesturing wildly and screaming obscenities. Shocked, I realized I was barrelling down a one-way street in the wrong direction. Like a wounded animal, I was conscious only of my need to get home.

Kay came home immediately after I called, and, with a hastily summoned ward member, administered to Lee. We still had a few minutes before we had to leave for the hospital, and I handed the camera to Kay. He took pictures until he ran out of film. Unspoken between us lay the dark fear that these would be the only pictures we would have of our baby.

For the next few days, I stayed at the hospital with Lee. Tests confirmed Dr. Venning's diagnosis of staph pneumonia, but that was all I knew. Dr. Venning wasn't one to volunteer information, and his intimidating manner discouraged me from asking questions. While he was obviously a brilliant diagnostic pediatrician, I missed the comforting familiarity of Dr. Strouth.

On the fourth morning, the antibiotics kicked in and Lee started to improve. Soon he was waving his arms and legs and making delighted baby noises at everyone who approached his hospital crib. A sociable little fellow, he soon became the pet of the pediatric floor.

Dr. Venning ordered a more sophisticated sweat test, and late that evening he came into Lee's room with the results. Without preamble he said, "The sweat test was negative for cystic fibrosis."

Dizzy with relief, I leaned against Lee's hospital crib. Our prayers had been answered. Soon we'd be taking our baby home, and the nightmare would be over. In my elation, I scarcely noticed that Dr. Venning wasn't sharing my excitement. Grim-faced, he was listening intently to Lee's lungs, ignoring my happy prattle.

When I entered Lee's room the next morning, I was surprised to see the lab technician repeating the test. "Why are you running it again?" I demanded anxiously. "Dr. Venning said it was negative."

"It was negative," the technician grumped sourly. "When a test's negative, it's negative, and him thinking it should be positive doesn't make it positive." I guessed that the "him" was Dr. Venning.

The second test, like the first, was negative. I thought that would be the end of it; but the following morning, the unhappy lab man was back. Grumbling that it was a waste of his time and our money, he gave Lee a third sweat test. It, too, was negative.

What was happening? It was obvious that, in spite of the negative test results, Dr. Venning still thought Lee had cystic fibrosis. My stomach tightened. Were we still in the nightmare?

At the end of the week, Dr. Venning released Lee from the hospital. Listening to his lungs a final time, he said, "He sounds clear, but I want to keep him on antibiotics for a while. Also, I'm arranging for the lab at St. Alphonsus Hospital to give him a sweat test."

Startled, I protested, "But all the tests except the screening test in your office have been negative!"

"They have," he agreed. "But I have a gut feeling about this. Every symptom points to cystic fibrosis, not an allergy."

A "Welcome Home" banner and gentle little pats and tender kisses greeted Lee as his siblings welcomed him home. I noted that the greeting was much more subdued than when I'd brought him home as a newborn. It was almost as if he were a fragile little guest.

A few days later in St. Alphonsus Hospital, Lee tested positive for the deadly disease, cystic fibrosis.

Numb with shock and despair, I spent the first few weeks in denial. Oh, I went through the motions. When Dr. Venning prescribed the pancreatic enzyme C/F children need to digest their food, I religiously sprinkled it on his food. Then, watching him screw up his face and gag when the enzyme turned his solids into a bitter, slimy mess, I would whisper, "Don't you worry, honey. Any day now the phone will ring, and it will be Dr. Venning telling us that it's all a mistake and that you don't have C/F after all."

Of course, the call didn't come; and gradually the numbness wore off and acceptance began. As it did, I remembered Elder Tanner's blessing. The Lord hadn't promised that Lee would be healed, but He had promised that He would give us wisdom and guidance.

But I must do my part. I must learn all there was to know about my son's disease. What I learned only added to my grief, for the bottom line in every pamphlet and medical article was the same. Cystic fibrosis was a disorder in which viscid, glue-like mucus impaired the digestive system and destroyed the lungs. There was no cure, and only a few children survived to school age. Lee's prognosis? He would be fortunate to live to be two.

Notwithstanding this grim forecast, at six months Lee looked surprisingly healthy. The enzymes were helping him digest his food, and the daily antibiotics were controlling his lung infections. He had gained weight and was busy trying to get the hang of crawling. So far, he had only succeeded in scooting backward on his stomach, a feat which delighted his buddy, Roger, who happily scooted backward with him.

The children adored their baby brother, and he ate it up, grabbing their hair and noses, laughing joyously at being the center of attention. He was so happy and alive that there were days when I could almost believe that it was all a mistake, that he couldn't possibly have a fatal disease.

In spite of Lee's seemingly good health, Dr. Venning felt it would be wise to have him examined by Dr. Jack M. Docter, who was the head of the Cystic Fibrosis Center in Seattle, Washington.

When we left Boise that November morning, the sky was overcast with the threat of winter, and we were concerned that we would run into bad roads. However, except for scattered snow flurries in the Blue Mountains of Oregon and a broken snow floor over the Snoquaimie Pass in Washington, the roads were dry.

Once at the Center, Lee was given another sweat test. While we waited for the results, I prayed for it to be negative. It was not to be. Lee tested positive, with a sodium count so high there was no possibility of error.

The diagnosis confirmed, we met with Dr. Docter. He was a

fairly tall man, on the thin side, with sad eyes and a kind smile. He told us that Lee was already suffering some lung damage, and recommended that he immediately start sleeping in a mist tent and begin a form of physical therapy called postural drainage. "The moisture produced in the mist tent liquifies the mucus in the airways and decreases its stickiness," he explained, "and clapping and vibrating the various lobes of the lung in postural drainage helps break the mucus loose so that the child can cough it out. We've found that these treatments, in many cases, extend the children's lives."

"In many cases," he'd said. But what about in Lee's case? Would it extend his life—and for how long? Months, years? And what would his quality of life be? The questions trembled unspoken on my lips. I sensed that there were no concrete answers.

When the cute young therapist with the blonde ponytail demonstrated postural drainage on a doll, it seemed simple enough. However, once home, I found there was a world of difference between clapping an inanimate object and a bucking, screaming six-month-old child with a mind of his own. Lee didn't mind too much when I bent him forward in my lap and clapped his back and chest, but when I draped him upside down over a pillow and started pounding, he declared war. Shrieking furiously, he hurled the toy in his hand across the room and fought to sit up. I wrestled with him, trying to force his head down with one hand, clap his chest with the other, and at the same time, keep the slippery pillow with him on it from slithering to the floor. Soon we were both drenched with perspiration. The first session ended abruptly when he threw up on my feet. And I was supposed to do this for forty-five minutes, three times a day?

As for Lee sleeping in a mist tent, that also sounded simple in the doctor's office. All we had to do was purchase a compressor and nebulizer, drape a piece of heavy plastic over the crib, stick Lee in it, turn a couple of knobs, and that was that.

Wrong! He was at an age when he was wary of unfamiliar objects—especially those that produced weird noises and vibrated all the doors and windows in the house.

Never big on lengthy solutions, it was difficult for me to slow down and acclimatize Lee to his new life a step at a time. But to hurry him was to invite disaster, and slowly I learned patience. It was a virtue that was to stand me in good stead during the years to come.

For the first week, I rocked him to sleep to the sound of the compressor. Once he was comfortable with that, I introduced him to the two nebulizers hanging inside his crib. Secure in my arms, he thought trying to catch the mist in his hands was a great game.

He was not so delighted when it came time for the real thing. For a few minutes I let him play as usual with the mist, but this time I didn't click it off when I laid him down. Instead, I pulled the heavy plastic over the top of the crib. Wide-eyed, he scrambled to the side, pulled himself to his feet, and clawed frantically at the plastic, roaring at the top of his lungs. He must have felt trapped in a cage with two mist-belching dragons! I was back to square one.

The tent was a miserable thing. Its heavy mist soaked his pajamas and made his sheets damp and clammy. Water condensed on the plastic and periodically plopped on his head. Startled awake, he would scramble to get away, only to bang his head on one of the nebulizers or, worse still, disturb the plastic, sending a shower of droplets cascading over him.

As time went by, however, I became a little smarter. I found that damp flannel doesn't feel nearly as cold and clammy as cotton, and that by cutting a hole in the top of the tent I could eliminate the condensation. Since mist is heavier than air, it still settled around him, providing the needed moisture.

So by trial and error, we adjusted to life with cystic fibrosis—much the same way, I suspect, as countless other families adjust to heartaches and problems that come into their lives.

Of his six siblings, Mary had to make the biggest physical adjustment, since she and Lee shared a room. She was a remarkably good sport. Without complaint, she endured the noisy equipment, Lee's coughing and crying out during the night, and my constant comings and goings—to say nothing of waking with damp hair every morning from the misty room!

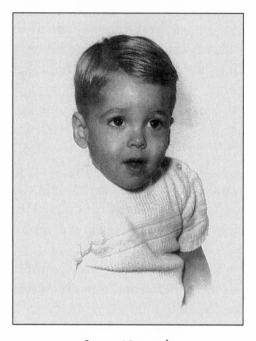

Lee at 10 months.

— 1964 —

I thought the winter months of 1964 would never end. Sub-zero temperatures kept the snow frozen on the ground, and arctic winds made it impossible for Steven and Roger to run their little-boy energy off outside. They were tired of their toys, and I no longer had time as in past winters to read them lengthy stories, help with puzzles, and sit with them in quiet play. Those precious hours had been usurped by postural drainages, cleaning and disinfecting equipment, and almost daily doctor appointments. Bored, the boys reduced the house and my nerves to shambles while I cared for Lee. After school, Stan added to my stress by practicing his newly acquired wrestling holds on his little brothers until one of them would end up hurt and crying.

While the boys were bouncing off the walls, the three girls, in stark contrast, were withdrawn and uncooperative. Our former lively after-school conversations had degenerated into a brief, "Hello, I'm home," thrown over a shoulder as they hurried to their rooms and disappeared behind closed doors. Before, they had helped around the house without complaint; but now, even my simplest requests were met with martyred looks and unlimited excuses until, too tired to insist, I snapped at them and did the task myself—only to become more tired and cross, continuing the vicious circle.

The only family member appearing to be untouched by the change in our lives was Kay, and that was probably because he was rarely at home. His work required at least some traveling during the month, and his responsibilities as bishop took him away many evenings as well as the greater part of each weekend. At times, he seemed more like a guest in our home than husband and father.

Bored little boys roughhousing, teen-aged daughters sulking over chores, a too-busy husband . . . it was a scenario no different from that found in thousands of other homes. But when added to my anxiety over Lee and my physical exhaustion, it was rapidly becoming more than I could handle.

The situation came to a head in April. For nearly four months, Lee had had one lung infection after another. During those bouts, I nursed him around the clock, afraid to sleep or leave him unattended for a minute. For he choked often, and when he did, I had to suck the strangling mucus from his throat with the small syringe I kept at his side.

The night began like countless other nights. Kay was at the church, and the children were sleeping. I sat beside Lee's crib, staring into the semi-darkness, listening to his harsh, labored breathing, tensely anticipating the next choking spell. It wasn't long in coming. Instantly, I was at his side, clapping his chest, the thick mist from the nebulizers boiling around my arm. He coughed, gagged, and sticky mucus filled his throat and mouth. Grabbing the syringe, I sucked it out. He twisted his head away, whimpered, and dozed off again.

I'd usurped Mary's bed for the duration and now I sagged down on it, propped myself against the piled-up pillows, and pulled an afghan over my legs. My head throbbed furiously. Perhaps if I closed my eyes for just a minute—

With a violent start, I awakened. The only sounds in the room were the chugging of the compressor and the hissing of the nebulizers. No sound of breathing came from the crib! Leaping up, I ripped away the plastic and scooped Lee into my arms. Immediately, his little body stiffened in protest, and he let out a startled cry.

Weak with relief, I leaned against the crib. He snuggled his face into my neck, his formerly raspy breathing now soft and even. For a long time, I just stood there, clutching him to my chest, my heart pounding. Then, with trembling hands, I eased him back into his tent.

Tiptoeing into the bathroom, I looked at my watch. It was 11:30 p.m. I had dozed off for less than fifteen minutes; during that short interval, Lee's breathing had eased. However, he could just as easily have choked. Guilt poured over me in nauseous waves. My knees buckled, and I slid to the floor. Hugging my legs, I buried my face in my arms and began to sob. Once started, I couldn't stop. I was still crying when Kay came home. Lifting me up, he carried me into our room. Holding me close, he stroked my hair and whispered, "It's going to be all right; everything's going to be all right."

But everything wasn't all right. The following Tuesday, Lee's pneumonia recurred, and I came down with a strep throat. My temperature soared to 104, and my doctor ordered an antibiotic and bed rest. The antibiotic I could do, the bed rest I could not. Someone had to care for Lee, and Kay was out of town.

The only thing that kept me going during that long week was knowing that on Friday night Kay would be home, and I could go to bed. However, he had scarcely entered the house when the phone rang. A ward member was in trouble and needed him. It couldn't wait.

When Kay arrived home at midnight, Lee had had another choking spell, and we were both crying. Looking drained, Kay took in the devastating scene and said, "I'm going to ask to be released as bishop."

"You're going to do *what?*" I croaked.

"I'm going to ask to be released," he repeated. "I can't travel on my job, do all that being a bishop entails, and give you the help you need at home. I feel guilty every time I walk out the door. You don't say anything, but I see the way you stiffen when you've counted on me being home, and the phone rings and I have to meet someone at the church. Not that I blame you," he added hastily. "You're so exhausted you're falling apart."

Head throbbing, throat on fire, I lashed out at him. "That's right," I cried. "Put a guilt trip on me! If you want out because you're tired, then ask to be released, but don't make me your excuse. I've toughed it out this long, and I can keep toughing it out. I've never once complained about the time you spend as bishop—well, maybe that one time when the bishopric took part in the Mutual's roadshow and you attended practices every night—but I've never resented the time you spend at meetings or with ward members. And I'm not, as you put it, falling apart. I have a strep infection, and I'm sick. Next week I'll be better. If you want to be released for reasons of your own, okay; but I'm not standing still for your blaming it on me."

My tirade ended, we stared at each other numbly. What was happening to us? An article I'd read in a C/F bulletin about the high incidence of divorce among C/F parents flashed through my mind, and my own vicious, undeserved words echoed in my ears. Was this how those couples' lives had started unraveling?

Kay broke the strained silence. "Let's not decide anything tonight," he said. "We're both exhausted."

I nodded. "Let's fast and pray about it first." We fasted the following day, and that night knelt together in prayer. When we rose, I felt good about the answer I had received. I knew there was still work for Kay to do as bishop. I also knew that the Lord was mindful of me and of our home situation. But I waited for Kay to speak.

In a quiet voice, he said, "I don't know why—there are certainly more qualified men than me in the ward—but, for whatever reason, for now, at least, I feel this is where the Lord wants me to serve." Putting his arms around me, he added, "It's going to be hard, especially for you, but I know that as long as we do our best, the Lord will see us through."

Before we left our room, Kay gave me a special blessing, asking that I be given the health, strength, and wisdom needed in fulfilling my calling as wife and mother during this season of my life.

Although we had told the children at the time of his diagnosis that Lee had cystic fibrosis and would need extra care, we didn't go into the details of the disease or Lee's prognosis. At the time, we felt there was no need for the sad cloud that hung over our lives to hang over their young, innocent ones. We wanted to let them enjoy their little brother without sadness, at least for a little while. Kay had felt for some weeks, however, that we had made a mistake. It wouldn't be long before the girls, at least, would overhear a conversation or read an article and know that C/F was a fatal disease. It was better that all the children hear it from us.

The night following our fast, Kay gathered the children around us in a family meeting. "We have a problem," he stated. "You know that Lee has cystic fibrosis and at times is very ill, but we've never really talked about C/F as a disease and how serious it is. I suppose that was because we wanted to protect you. We were wrong. Lee's having C/F is a family matter, and we need to face it as a family."

When he explained the seriousness of cystic fibrosis and that most C/F children only survive a few years, Mary sucked in her breath. Six pairs of stricken eyes were riveted on their father's face.

"We're fortunate with Lee," Kay continued, attempting to sound positive. "He was diagnosed early, and the doctors have taught us how to help him. Our job now is to take care of him and keep him as well as we can until researchers find a cure. That may take them a long time; and in the meantime, Lee will sometimes be very ill like he's been the past few months, and other times he'll be fine. But even when he's well, he still needs a lot of special care. That's where you children and I come in. Your mother has worn herself out trying to take care of him and still keep our lives running smoothly. Now it's time we all pitched in and did our share."

After their father's explanation, a miraculous change came over the three girls. It was as if a dam of misunderstanding had burst. Thirteen-year-old Patty, who usually hid her feelings deep within herself, brushed my cheek with her lips and in a choked voice said, "I'm sorry I've given you a hard time when you've asked for help after school. It was just that my friends always got to watch TV or talk on the phone when they came home, but I always had to pitch right in and do chores. I guess I felt picked on."

Mary and Irene nodded in agreement. "I didn't feel like I had any time for myself," Mary added. "Unless I had a baby-sitting job for that evening, the minute I walked into the house you were after me to fold the clothes, tend the baby, or help get dinner. It seemed like the more I did, the more you wanted me to do. I didn't think it was fair that I had to come home and do your work when you'd been home all day."

And I had felt like a martyr! Well, at least now I knew why they rushed to their rooms as soon as they came home from school!

But it was Irene's reaction that was the eye-opener. Only then did I realize how mistaken we'd been not to confide in them earlier. "When you stopped laughing and kidding with me," she cried, "I thought I'd done something bad, and you didn't love me anymore."

When Kay asked the children how they thought they could help, immediate offers were forthcoming—for the most part realistic ones from the girls, and wildly impractical ones from the boys. I found myself swallowing a lump in my throat as the dark cloud of misunderstanding lifted, and closed doors were opened and feelings shared and resolved.

Of course, as time went on, we often fell short of our good intentions. The girls grew tired of doing extra chores, the boys forgot their promises to be "good," and I was grouchy for no good reason. Nevertheless, we had learned some valuable lessons—not the least of which was that it's seldom in children's best interests to protect them from family problems. They sense something is wrong, and not knowing what it is only adds to their confusion and fears.

During the summer, as Lee's health improved and I settled into a routine, I experienced an unexpected side effect of Lee's illness: I was lonely. I had been released from my calling in the Relief Society to care for Lee, and I had put my community activities on hold. Except for Lee's appointments with the doctor, I seldom left home. Oh, I talked occasionally with my friends on the phone, but it wasn't the same. Their lives were continuing on as before, while mine had detoured into a frightening new world governed by cystic fibrosis. Listening to them chatter about their activities made me feel even lonelier.

During those dark days, I yearned to talk to someone who lived in my same world, and for months I searched unsuccessfully for another C/F family. Then, strictly by chance, I ran into a C/F mother who, in turn, led me to two others. It was not long before I was communicating with dozens of parents living in all areas of Idaho.

In the beginning, our little network was solely an emotional support group, but soon we realized we must look beyond our personal grief and do more than commiserate with each other. Rather than remain passive victims, we needed to do battle against this merciless disease. Only then would our feelings of helplessness be eased.

And so it was that three days after Christmas, the parents of four C/F children and a few supporters met in our home, and the Gem State Cystic Fibrosis Chapter* was born. Little did we dream at that meeting that the chapter would grow to include branches throughout the state. We not only met our immediate goal, which was to get C/F under the Crippled Children Services, but we instituted programs to educate the general public as well as many in the medical community about the then little-known disease.

Chapter members in cities and farming communities throughout the state staged fund-raising events, sending thousands of dollars to the C/F Foundation for research. Recognizing the desperate need for a C/F Clinic in the Boise/Nampa area, we spearheaded the drive for the first C/F Clinic in the area. And with each C/F article we wrote, with each speech and interview

---

*Later renamed the Idaho Cystic Fibrosis Chapter.

we gave, and with each dollar we raised for research, our morale improved. We were fighting back.

Lee in his mist tent.

— 1965 —

In late spring, Kay was released as bishop. I recalled the traumatic night a year earlier when we had fasted and prayed about asking for his release, and both of us had received the impression that he was to continue to serve—that there was still someone whose life he was to touch as a bishop. The evening of his release, he worried aloud as to whether or not he had fulfilled that assignment.

Years later, in a crowded restaurant, a ward member who had long since moved away threw her arms around Kay and started to weep. She told him that his counsel during the last months he was bishop had changed her life; she had progressed from total inactivity to becoming a regular temple patron. Perhaps she was the one whose heart Kay was to touch; I don't know. I do know, however, that during that extra year we learned a powerful lesson. We learned that if we have the faith to do what the Lord asks of us, He'll give us the blessings we need to accomplish it—and more.

Lee turned two in May, the age his doctors had predicted he would never reach. With a birthday hat perched on his head and eyes glistening with excitement, he looked like any other two-year-old celebrating his birthday. He acted like one, too—especially when he seized a fistful of birthday cake and crammed it into his mouth before I could do a thing!

With silky blond hair, huge hazel eyes, and delicate features, he looked like an angel; but, in truth, he was a rough-and-tumble lad, liking nothing better than to wrestle with his brothers. Yet he was marvelously adaptable, and went good-naturedly from being roughed up by them to playing dress-up with his sisters, even allowing them to outfit him in a ruffled tutu with a lace doily on top of his head.

How we loved him! When we were misunderstood, he was there with his sticky hugs and gooey kisses. When we needed a laugh, his cheerful antics provided it. When our arms were empty, he filled them. None of us could imagine our lives without him.

In August, we jumped in our old station wagon and drove to the family cabin on the shore of Payette Lake in McCall, Idaho. Kay and I had spent our honeymoon there, and nearly every year since we had returned to this lovely spot for our vacation. The cabin was small and borderline primitive, but we loved it.

As soon as the car stopped, the children bolted down the path that led to the beach, where they introduced their little brother to the joys of vacationing at the cabin. Holding Lee's hands, Roger and Steven raced him barefoot up and down the warm, sandy beach until he was breathless. Irene taught him to shovel sand into a bucket, and Patty taught him that dumping it on an unsuspecting sunbather was a "no-no." Secure in a life jacket, he let Mary lead him into the shallow water of the beach, shuddering deliciously as the cold water rippled over his feet. When a wave from a passing boat unexpectedly engulfed him to his waist, he scrambled into her arms, and together they laughed and bobbed in the waves.

Lee's greatest joy, however, was the boat. No sooner did we return from a ride than he was tugging at his father's hand, begging to go again. Sitting high in my lap, he laughed and shouted into the wind as we bounced and bucked over the waves.

Next best were the evening campfires on the beach, especially the marshmallows Stan toasted for him. It didn't concern him that Stan occasionally caught one on fire or allowed one to dip into the ashes. He loved them, ashes and all.

For the first day or so at the cabin, I had to consciously work at not being overprotective. Kay and I knew how important it was that this first vacation at the cabin with Lee be as much fun for the other children as it had always been. The relief and joy on their faces as we went from one traditional activity to another was testimony that we had succeeded.

As always, we picked huckleberries, and I made huckleberry pancakes and pies. We explored new paths in the woods and swam in the lake. Drifting in the boat, we counted osprey nests in the snags along the shoreline and waved to friends on the beach. Kay and the children water skied, and every night we ate s'mores and told jokes and stories around the campfire.

The only evidence of any difference between this vacation and past ones was the conversion of the old playpen into a mist tent, and the drainages that were worked around the fun times.

At the end of the week, we returned home rejuvenated. The vacation had been a wonderful tonic for all of us—especially for the children, who, I suspect, had wondered if life would ever be the same again.

We had hoped to repeat the experience over the long Labor Day weekend, but it was not to be; Lee developed a lung infection the week before we were to go. Rather than canceling the trip, we decided that Kay would take the other children while I cared for Lee at home. Accordingly, Kay hurried home from work on Friday night, hooked up the boat, and they all piled into the car. Lee and I waved from the porch as they headed down the street.

Suddenly, it hit Lee that the boat was going, and he was not. He dropped my hand and tore after it, screaming, "Boat, boat, wait for Lee!" I ran after him, but before I could reach him, he had collapsed in the middle of the street. He lay there, chest heaving, trying to suck oxygen into pneumonia-filled lungs. As I carried him to the house, a convulsive coughing spell left him blue and exhausted. Once inside, I cradled him in my arms and rocked him for a long time. Gradually, his sobs faded into sad little hiccups.

I cooked his favorite foods for dinner, but he pushed them away. Nor did he show any interest in his toys. Following the evening drainage, I rocked him again, singing him songs and reading him funny stories. A brief smile would occasionally touch his lips and soften his tight little face; but for the most part, he lay spiritless in my arms, clutching his blanket. When at last his eyelids drooped in sleep, I tucked him into his mist tent and crept into Mary's bed beside it. There, I stared into the darkness, tears rolling silently down my cheeks until finally I, too, fell asleep.

—1966—

The end of January saw us once more in Dr. Docter's office in Seattle. The good news was that, while small for his age, Lee was growing satisfactorily, his heart was good, he had no polyps, and his liver appeared normal.

The bad news was that his emphysema was more pronounced. Only two and a half years old, his baby chest was already noticeably barreled. In spite of the mist tent, postural drainage, and aggressive antibiotic therapies, the disease was continuing its deadly march, methodically destroying his lungs as it progressed.

Sensing my hopelessness, the doctor quickly assured me that although Lee's emphysema had spread, his lungs were "not that bad." How bad "not that bad" was, I didn't know. Nevertheless, the disease had progressed; and he added mucomyst inhalation to Lee's treatments. Mucomyst, a mucolytic agent, would thin the mucus and make it easier for him to cough it up.

At the conclusion of our visit, Dr. Docter asked if we had any questions, and I hurriedly whipped out the list I'd prepared before leaving Boise. The first ones were strictly medical, and he dealt comfortably with those. The next questions were hard for me to ask and even more difficult for the doctor to answer, for they centered on his prognosis for Lee. His demeanor changed, and when he spoke, it was as if he were repeating carefully-rehearsed words—the same words he had spoken to countless other C/F parents who had asked him the same impossible questions, words meant to encourage without building up false hope.

I was struck again by this man's eyes. How old and sad they looked. I crumpled the list of questions and shoved it back into my purse. They were questions he could not possibly answer the way I longed to have them answered, and it wasn't fair to ask them of him.

Back in Boise, I contacted Dr. Venning. He had received Dr. Docter's letter recommending the use of mucomyst, and, as a pediatric allergist, he was not happy. After filling me in on all the things that could happen should Lee have a bad allergic reaction, he left the decision as to its use up to Kay and me. We agonized over it that evening without coming to a decision; and when Kay left town on business the next morning, he left the choice up to me. That which I had prayed would never happen, had happened. I was caught between differing opinions of the two doctors I most highly respected.

Dr. Venning was a brilliant allergist, totally committed to his patients, and a miracle worker as far as Lee was concerned. Yet, I wondered if that very expertise was causing him to be too hesitant about using a substance that could conceivably extend Lee's life. Dr. Docter had used it extensively on C/F patients without problems; and, since he felt it might slow down the damage to Lee's lungs, how could we not try it?

Still, I hesitated. My mother had spent the greater part of my college years in and out of hospitals because of an allergic reaction to a seemingly innocuous drug, eventually ending up at the Mayo Clinic in critical condition. Since then, I had been paranoid about drug-related allergies.

All day I seesawed back and forth, one hour feeling strongly that we should use the new therapy, and the next hour feeling just as strongly that we must not. I prayed silently all day, but when nightfall came I was no closer to a decision than I had been that morning.

At midnight, I crept into Lee's room and knelt at the side of his mist tent. I thanked the Lord for guidance received over the years and pleaded for that guidance again, asking that if my decision to go with the mucomyst therapy was correct, I would have peace of mind. I went back to bed and immediately fell asleep. The decision was made, and I felt it was the correct one.

Even so, Lee's introduction to mucomyst was a near tragedy—

not because of an allergic reaction, but because of the incompetence of the equipment salesman! Dr. Venning, still concerned about possible side effects, had arranged for Lee's first treatment to be given in his office so he could be at Lee's side in case of a reaction. The salesman met us there.

Lee sat on my lap and surveyed the assembled equipment warily. Because breathing was difficult for him at best, I was afraid he would fight the mask; and I regretted not having asked that the first treatment be postponed until I'd introduced it to him gradually. These treatments were going to be a permanent part of his therapy regimen, and I couldn't afford to have them turn into a battle of wills.

Dr. Venning carefully measured and poured the mucomyst, distilled water, and isuprel into the small nebulizer. The isuprel would dilate the bronchial tubes and allow the mucus thinning agent to penetrate more deeply into the airways.

With everything in readiness, the salesman turned on the compressor and slipped the mask on Lee's face. Before I could react, Lee's hand shot up, ripped the mask off and hurled it, still connected to the nebulizer, across the room.

Dr. Venning gaped in disbelief. This was a far different Lee from the one who stoically allowed himself to be probed, thumped, and poked with a needle every time he entered this building. The salesman flushed angrily, turned off the compressor, and retrieved the mask and nebulizer.

"Maybe we should take a minute and get him used to the mask before you turn on the machine," I suggested, knowing full well it was going to take longer than a minute to get Lee used to having a mask on his face.

"Give in to him this time, and he'll think he can get away with it next time," the salesman answered curtly. Mask in hand, he clicked the compressor on, and once more the malodorous mucomyst vapor hissed into the air. Before I could protest, the salesman had forcibly imprisoned Lee's head in one of his big, hairy hands, while with the other he pressed the mask hard into

Lee's face, completely covering his nose and mouth. Using his ham-like arm, he warded off Lee's frantic attempts to yank it away. Except for an initial smothered cry, Lee fought silently with all the strength of his little body. Again and again, he arched his back and threw himself frantically against my chest, trying to dislodge the mask. The salesman only held his head tighter and pressed the mask harder into his face. Simultaneously, Dr. Venning and I grabbed the salesman's hands and wrenched them away.

For a few seconds, all Lee could do was gulp for air. Then, shrieking hysterically, he scrambled around in my lap and buried his face under my chin, his arms clenched around my neck. He was dripping with sweat, and his little heart shook his body. Sickened, I could only hold him tightly and whisper tearfully, "You're okay, Lee. You're okay."

Gradually, he calmed down and loosened his grip enough for us to see his face. The skin on his forehead and around his eyes was speckled with red dots where the capillaries had ruptured. His face was a grayish blue, and the mask had carved a deep ridge around his nose and mouth.

Dr. Venning sucked in his breath at the sight. "That's terrible, just terrible," he said, looking as sick as I felt. Whirling, he faced the salesman and demanded, "Are you sure he could breathe with the mask pressed that tightly against his face? He acted like he was being smothered, and he certainly looks like he has been!"

Testily, the salesman replied, "Oh, he could breathe all right. The compressor pumps air through the nebulizer into the mask. He threw a tantrum and held his breath."

Unconvinced, Dr. Venning picked up the apparatus and examined it more closely. Seeing Dr. Venning pick up the dreaded mask, Lee clutched me tightly around the neck again, sobbing forlornly, "Wanna go home now."

"You damned idiot," Dr. Venning exploded. "There are no holes for the air to get out. The compressor forced air through the nebulizer into the mask all right, but Lee couldn't breathe out because you held it so tightly to his face. You damned near killed that baby!"

A week passed before I tried introducing Lee to the mask again. Then, it was only to slip an adult-sized one on my own face while Lee watched from a safe distance. Riveted by the sight, he stood his ground until I started walking slowly toward him. Then he took off like a shot, dropping to all fours in his haste to scramble up the stairs to the upper level of our split-level home.

Removing the mask, I went after him. I found him in the bathroom, scrunched into a little ball, hiding behind the toilet. I held my hands out to him, but he eyed me suspiciously and refused to budge. Finally, enticed by a cookie, he edged his way out; and I rocked him until he relaxed. Clearly, my strategy had backfired, and I would have to come up with a new plan.

The next morning I laid the mask on the couch. Looking at it warily, he gave it a wide berth for a few hours. But in the afternoon, when he needed more room to line up his little cars, he picked it up and contemptuously threw it on the floor, where it lay ignored. That evening, when it was time to put away his toys, he tossed it with them into the toy box.

Once his fear of touching the mask was gone, we graduated to giving Irene's child-sized doll a treatment. I put water in the nebulizer, placed the mask on the doll's face, and turned on the compressor. At first, Lee refused to come near the doll. However, curiosity won him over, and soon he was sitting on the floor beside me, holding the doll on his lap, trying to catch the mist in his fingers.

While he gave the doll a treatment, I periodically placed my cupped hand over his nose and mouth, saying, "Lee's treatment" and removing it before he had time to protest. After a few days, I slipped a child-sized mask on his face. Busy giving the masked doll its treatment, he didn't object. It was now time to get him accustomed to the smell of the mucomyst.

While he watched, I made a big show of measuring the mucomyst and isuprel into the nebulizer. This time, we were going to give the doll a "real" treatment. I snapped on the switch, and he crinkled his nose slightly at the smell, but didn't object. He held the doll for a few seconds until, suddenly bored with the whole thing, he pushed it into my lap and said, "You do it." He left me sitting in the middle of the floor, administering a very expensive drug to a doll, while he went upstairs to play with Roger!

That evening, with a picture book in his hands and Roger sitting companionably beside him, Lee sat quietly inhaling the mucus-thinning agent while I pointed to the cow that moos, the kitty that meows, and the dog that barks. He had no adverse reactions to the drug.

In May, we celebrated his third birthday. Mother drove up from Twin Falls, and Kay's parents came over for dinner. For months, Lee had looked forward to this day—the day we'd promised him he would graduate from the crib to a regular bed because, as he reminded us often and loudly, "Big boys, three, do not sleep in cribs!"

As soon as the birthday cake and ice cream were consumed, the entire family trooped up the stairs to the bedroom he still shared with Mary. Dancing with excitement, he handed tools to his father, and soon the crib was dismantled and the new single bed set up. Pat smoothed out the last wrinkle in the new beige and blue cowboy spread; and Lee, not able to contain himself another second, climbed on it, grinning up at us with triumphant eyes. Then he spotted Kay carrying in a tent frame and canopy.

"What's that?" he demanded suspiciously, sitting up and pointing at the assembly.

"It's your new mist tent," his father answered cheerfully. "Jump out, and I'll show you how it works. This part goes under your new mattress. And this part"—he took hold of the plastic—"makes you a brand new tent. Pretty neat, huh?"

The anticipation drained from Lee's face. His lower lip quivered, and tears threatened to spill from his eyes. "Big kids don't sleep in a tent," he announced, blinking hard. "They sleep in a bed like hers." He indicated Mary's bed. "I'm this many now." He held up three fingers. "Only babies sleep in mist tents, not big boys like me."

Too late, Kay and I realized that Lee equated sleeping in a mist tent with sleeping in a crib. Being the baby of the family, he must have thought all little people slept in mist tents.

Unanswered questions flashed through my mind. What about the inhalation treatments, the shots, the blood tests, the postural drainages? In the innocence of childhood, did he think they, too, were a part of being "little"? How would we tell him this was the way his life was always going to be—and when should we tell him? We had used the words "cystic fibrosis" freely, making no effort to hide the fact he had the disease. But when and how were we going to tell him its implications?

Diplomatically, the three grandparents excused themselves, but not before I saw tears in my mother's eyes. In a sudden rush of understanding, I knew they were for me, her "baby" daughter, as well as for her little grandson.

Kay and I stared at each other, at a loss for words. But not the boys. Just as in many times past, they saved the day.

"Hey, Lee, all right!" Steve exclaimed. "Look at that neat tent; what a super hideout!"

"Bring your race cars up here, Lee," Stan echoed. "This will make a cool parking garage."

Lee wavered slightly; his brothers had hoodwinked him before, and he eyed them skeptically. But it was Roger who provided the clincher when he unexpectedly burst into tears and demanded, "How come Lee always gets to sleep in a tent, and I never do? It's not fair! He should have to take turns."

At that, Lee scrambled to his feet and stood belligerently between his bed and his brother, declaring emphatically, "It's my birthday bed, not yours."

That night when I tucked him into his new bed, I asked, "Lee, do you know why you sleep in a tent and Roger doesn't?"

He shook his head.

"It's because you have cystic fibrosis, and sleeping in a mist tent makes it easier for you to breathe," I explained.

Tired from his big day, he only nodded sleepily and said, "Oh."

Small though it was, I had taken my first conscious step toward acquainting him with the demands of his disease. Somehow, we had to teach him that while those demands were nothing to hide or be ashamed of, neither could they be neglected with impunity. Standing beside his bed, I turned on the compressor and watched the tent quickly fill with cool, damp mist, obscuring him from my view. Silently I prayed, "Help me be a good teacher."

In the fall, Mary started dating a rather popular senior in high school. He was a nice boy, and I felt comfortable with her dating him. However, one night when she tapped on our bedroom door to check in, her voice sounded strained. I slipped into a robe and followed her into her room.

We chatted a few minutes about the dance before I asked if something was wrong. She started to shake her head, but then her face crumpled and she blurted out, "His mother doesn't want him to date me anymore."

I stared at her. Why would any mother object to her son dating my lovely daughter? My spine stiffened with indignation.

"She told him that we might fall in love, and if we married our children would have C/F like Lee."

For a moment I was speechless. "Did you tell him you would both have to carry the gene to have a C/F baby, and then the chances are only one in four?" I asked when I could speak.

"No, I didn't," she replied indignantly, wiping away her tears with a defiant gesture. "I told him I would consider myself lucky to have a baby as special as Lee, whether he had C/F or not. Then I got out of the car and came into the house. His mother needn't worry about me dating her boy again!"

Looking into my eyes, she added, "I meant it about Lee. Even if he can only stay with us a few years, I wouldn't trade the time we've had with him for anything."

I put my arms around her. But inside me was the unanswered question, *Are there other parents out there who are going to be unwilling to let their sons or daughters date my children because they have a C/F brother?* A cold chill coursed down my spine.

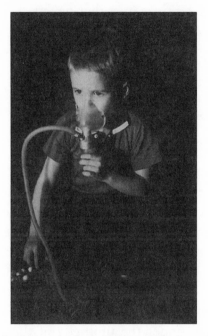

Inhalation therapy—an important part of Lee's medical regimen.

—1967—

At the first of the year, we replaced the jet type nebulizers in Lee's mist tent with a newly marketed ultrasonic one. This one not only produced a finer mist that penetrated deeper into Lee's airways, but it was more user-friendly. A single unit that stood beside Lee's bed with only a flex tube extending into the canopy, it was wonderfully quiet.

In fact, it was so quiet that for the first few nights none of us slept. We had to get used to a mist tent all over again, only this time in reverse. Instead of adjusting to a chugging compressor and rattling doors and windows, we had to adjust to normal nighttime sounds. We hadn't heard a car door slam, the wail of an emergency vehicle, or a dripping faucet at night since Lee started mist tent therapy. Now we heard all of these, plus the eerie, unidentified creaks and groans emitting from the house itself. We'd forgotten how creepy a quiet house could be!

In April, I was asked to be the stake MIA Young Women's president. It was a major calling. At that time, not only the youth, but also the young adults, young marrieds, and special interest group fell under the umbrella of the Mutual program. The stake Mutual was responsible for the Saturday night youth dances, talent contests, dramatic productions, speech contests, special stake evenings for the girls, and sports and camping programs. Besides these stake activities, there were leadership meetings to prepare and wards to be visited weekly. In other words, it was a calling that could not be taken lightly!

My first instinct was to decline the call. How could I give it the required time and still care for Lee and our other six children? Besides, I was deeply involved in our Cystic Fibrosis Chapter. In the fall, we were going to conduct our first door-to-door fund raising campaign, and it was important that it be successful. I rationalized that there were any number of women in the stake better qualified for the Mutual position, but there were few in the community willing to devote as much time and energy as I was to fighting C/F. Wasn't that important, too?

Then, in the midst of my deliberations came the self-serving thought, "If I accept this calling and do my best, maybe the Lord will repay me by keeping Lee alive until a cure is found."

No sooner had the unworthy thought entered my mind, however, than I recalled the words of a relative who had lost his daughter in a drowning accident. "All the way to the hospital," he related, "I promised the Lord that if He would let her live, I would devote my entire life to His service. Later, waiting outside the emergency room, I knew that my prayer, although it came from a breaking heart, was wrong. I sought a quiet place and there I uttered the most difficult prayer of my life. I told the Lord that although I would give my own life gladly for this child, not my will, but His be done. Regardless of the outcome, I would serve and worship Him with all my heart."

His little daughter slipped away, but her father served faithfully as a bishop and later in a stake presidency until his own death many years later.

If I accepted the call, it had to be because I was willing to serve unconditionally. After several days of weeping, fasting, and praying, I accepted. I knew the Lord was well aware of my family situation and the care Lee demanded. He also knew my personal weaknesses and limitations, which were many. If knowing this, He still wanted me, how could I not accept?

And thanks to the Lord's blessings, an outstanding stake board, and a supportive husband and children, never once during the eight years I served did I regret the decision—well, maybe a few times at girls' camp!

During that summer, five of our support group's C/F children died—children I had grown to love as my own. As death followed death, I plummeted into a deep depression, accompanied by an irrational panic that bordered on paranoia. Every day I examined Lee's fingers and toes for clubbing, a tell-tale sign of lack of oxygen to his extremities. I measured his chest and wondered if it was larger because of natural growth or because of advancing emphysema. When he came in from play short of breath, his lips blue, my heart pounded erratically until I calmed down and realized he had been running hard in the cold and was not cyanotic.

Adding to my trauma was the roller-coaster ride generated by sensationalized reports of "major breakthroughs" and of controls "just around the corner." After each bitter disappointment, I resolved never to get my hopes up again. Yet, how quickly my resolve faded in my desperation to believe that this time, surely, the cure was for real.

When Lee was first diagnosed with cystic fibrosis, I naively assumed that all C/F specialists agreed on treatments. But now I knew differently, and many nights I laid awake staring at the ceiling, comparing treatments prescribed by his doctors with that of other doctors, wondering if a different medication or a different type of treatment would be more effective, my mind darting this way and that. Nothing was ever resolved, and often dawn found me standing by his bed, my cheeks wet with tears.

When I did doze off, there were the nightmares. They were always the same. It was dusk; and with Lee heavy in my arms, I was stumbling through a blinding blizzard, fighting to reach the crest of a mountain. My arms, straining under his weight, lost their feeling, and I was terrified that I would drop him and he would be lost forever. I sensed that time was running out and I tried to hurry, but my movements were slow, as if I were in slow motion. As I climbed, I was conscious of small mounds beneath the drifted snow, and with horror I realized that they were the bodies of children who had fallen victim to the mountain. I tightened my grip on Lee and screamed for help. In the distance, I caught a glimmer of light; and for a few seconds hope filled me with renewed energy. But almost immediately the light went out.

I lost my sense of direction in the swirling snow and stood immobilized. Darkness enveloped us.

I always awoke at that point, heart pounding, drenched in sweat. The nightmare, of course, was not one of conquering a wintry mountain. It was the nightmare of cystic fibrosis. The storm of conflicting opinions swirled about me, obscuring my way, confusing my sense of direction. Promises of a control, like a light, would beckon, tantalize, and then disappear, leaving dark hopelessness in their wake. Yet scaling that mountain was Lee's only hope.

During the day, thoughts of death—Lee's death—consumed me. I became obsessed with a need to burn everything about him into my memory: how his face lit up when he laughed, the happy inflection of his voice when he spoke, the warm pressure of his spontaneous hugs, the feel of his kisses on my cheek. I wondered if this was what a mental breakdown felt like; and I often searched my face in the mirror, surprised that the calm blue eyes staring back at me gave no hint of anguish.

Ashamed of my weakness, I went to great lengths to conceal my depression from family and friends. When I talked too brightly or laughed too loudly, thankfully, no one noticed. Once, I almost shared my feelings with a friend when I saw her at the grocery store. We exchanged a few pleasantries, and she inquired about Lee. I told her he was fine and related a funny comment he had made. She laughed and then unexpectedly said, "You're so brave, Karma, always smiling with a funny story to tell. I wouldn't be able to stand it if it were my child."

Impulsively, I started to confide in her, to share my fears. "I'm really not brave at all," I said. "In fact, right now I'm a basket case."

"Oh, really?" She looked confused. "But didn't you say Lee is doing well?"

"He is," I agreed. "That's what's so crazy. I don't understand what's happening to me."

Clearly uncomfortable, she glanced at her watch. "Oh, look at the time," she said hurriedly. "I have to run, but give me a call one of these days, and we'll have a nice, long talk." She gave my shoulders a squeeze and added, "Remember, dear, into each life some rain must fall."

After one particularly bad night, I decided to talk to an older woman I knew, a woman who had had much tragedy in her life, yet still moved forward with faith and dignity. If anyone could help me, she could. However, as I lifted my hand to knock on her door, I began to cry; and, ashamed of my tears, I ran back to the sanctuary of the car. Laying my head on the steering wheel, I sobbed hopelessly, engulfed in such black despair that for a fleeting moment I wanted to smash myself into oblivion.

Shocked that I had entertained such a thought for even an instant, I started the car and headed out of the city toward the desert. There, where only the wind and the sagebrush could hear, I poured out my heart to my Lord, pleading for His help.

I don't know how long I had been there when into my mind came the picture of Roger and Lee as I'd watched them at play the day before. They were playing Marines and were dressed in Kay's old World War II uniforms. Kay's heavy flight jacket hung down past Lee's knees, and a Marine hat clung precariously to the back of his head. With a long stick rifle slung over his shoulder, a canteen on his hip, and a pack on his back, he struggled manfully to keep up with "Captain Roger" as they marched around and around the yard.

Suddenly he stepped in a small hole and fell heavily to the ground. He labored to get up but couldn't regain his footing. His burden was too heavy. Exhausted and helpless under the weight, he tearfully called for help. Immediately, Roger was at his side. He removed the pack and canteen from his little brother, heaved the heavy pack onto his own shoulders, and tied the canteen around his own waist. Pulling Lee to his feet, he crammed the Marine hat back on his head, and with a commanding, "Forward, march," they tramped together around the yard again, this time with Roger's hand at Lee's elbow, ready to steady him should he stumble again.

Like Lee, I was struggling with burdens I could no longer bear alone. And there in the desert, my Savior heard my cry and took them upon Himself. This is not to say that my depression immediately disappeared, never to return. But it lessened and no longer threatened to destroy me.

I practiced replacing destructive thoughts with positive ones. Where formerly I had visualized myself weeping over a tiny grave, now I pictured myself applauding at a college graduation. When Lee tugged on my skirt and asked, "Guess what I'm going to be when I grow up?", instead of avoiding his eyes and later weeping in my room, I drew him into my lap, and we laughed and talked about how much fun it would be to pilot a jet.

A well-meaning friend told me that I must face Lee's death head on, or when it came I wouldn't be "prepared." But how does one prepare for the death of a child? By allowing the specter of death to be a constant companion? By allowing its sulking presence to annihilate the laughter of today? I think not. I believe preparing for death is to live each moment to the fullest so that at the end there are no regrets.

In September, Mary left home to attend Brigham Young University. Lee had thought it would be fun to have their room all to himself, but now he found it lonely and often talked one of his brothers into sleeping in her bed to keep him company. Mary had been like a second mother to him. Often at night when I hurried to their room in response to a choking cough or frightened cry, I would find her already bent over him, crooning softly and patting his back. She would nod to indicate that all was well, and I would return to my room, a lump in my throat, touched by the solicitous love she showed her baby brother.

—1968—

I knew that one day Lee would ask the inevitable question, and for years I had carefully rehearsed an answer in my mind. However, I didn't dream it would come so quickly—and certainly not when we were surrounded by a half dozen little neighborhood friends helping to celebrate his fifth birthday!

Busy dishing up ice cream, I didn't see or hear what Lee did to trigger her rage, but suddenly from the back yard came a little girl's high-pitched scream. "I hate you, Lee Belnap, and I'm glad you've got something terrible and are going to die."

Deathly silence reigned until Lee, momentarily shocked speechless, found his voice and shrieked back, "You're a liar, a good for nothin' girl liar. I don't have nothin', and I'm not going to die."

"You are so!" To clinch the argument, she added triumphantly, "My mama said you are, so *there*."

"Your mother's a liar, too, then," he roared back, "and your mom had better be careful what she says about me, or my mom will go over and punch her lights out. So there, yourself!"

With that, the back door flew open, and Lee, followed by his friends, tumbled into the kitchen where I stood immobilized. Face scarlet, eyes black with anger, he demanded, "Tell her I haven't got somethin' terrible that's going to make me die. Tell her she's a liar!" Tears filled his eyes, and sudden doubt made his voice quiver. "I'm not going to die, am I?" he begged. "Make her take back what she said!" Grabbing me around the legs, he hid his crumbling face in my skirt.

In the background, I heard a little boy's angry whisper, "Susie*, you're in big trouble now. I'm gonna tell Mama you told, and you're gonna get a good whupping."

---

*Name changed.

At this, Susie began to wail; and as if on cue, the other two little girls joined in. Meanwhile, the little boys stared at me with round, questioning eyes. Leaning over, I held Lee close. I felt his heart pounding through his thin cotton shirt, and his breathing was ragged as he repeated, "Have I got somethin' terrible? Am I going to die?"

Clearly, this was neither the time nor the place for my carefully prepared speech. Instead, I motioned for the children to sit down on the floor; and, not trusting my suddenly weak legs, I slid to the floor with them, Lee's face still buried deep in my lap.

The three little girls stopped their caterwauling. I beckoned to Susie, who stood poised at the door ready to flee, to come and sit by me. She hesitated for a minute and then reluctantly came over and sat stiffly on the floor beside me. I put my free arm around her.

"Okay," I said, buying some time, "let's talk."

Not knowing quite how to begin, I turned to Susie and asked, "What terrible thing do you think Lee has?"

For a moment she didn't answer. Then in a faltering voice, she said, "I dunno, but Mama said it makes him cough a lot, and he's going to die." She eyed her brother nervously. Obviously, she had been warned at home not to repeat her parents' conversations about Lee.

At that, Lee pulled his face out of my lap, scrambled up, and leaned over her, fists clenched. "It's 'cause I've got C/F that I cough. But I don't have nothin' bad. I just have C/F. That's all I have, isn't it, Mom?" Frightened little boy eyes searched mine.

"You just have C/F," I agreed. "Nothing else."

"And I'm not going to die, am I?" In spite of his words, uncertainty clouded his face, and his body tensed while he waited for my reply.

"Not for a long time, Lee, and not before you're ready," I assured him.

Looking into the little faces surrounding me, I saw disbelief in many of the children's eyes, and I wondered how much they'd overheard in their homes. As much as I longed to end the conversation, I knew for Lee's sake I had to make them comfortable with him and with cystic fibrosis. Addressing them as casually as possible, I said, "Sometimes people don't know much about C/F, and they get all mixed up like Susie did."

"I didn't get mixed up!" Susie might be frightened, but she wasn't backing down. "Mama said Lee's going to die," she maintained stubbornly, "and he is!"

"All of us die sometime, Susie," I answered. "You, me, Josh, Tracy, all of us. That's how we get back to our Heavenly Father. But," I added briskly, getting to my feet in hopes of ending the conversation, "that's a long time from now. Heavenly Father needs us to do lots of things here first."

"Mama says Lee has to sleep in an awful bed that's wet all the time," Susie persisted, "and have shots and all kinds of bad things done to him."

For a moment, I was tempted to take Lee's advice and go over and actually punch her mother's lights out!

"Aw, you and your mom are nuts," one of the little boys said, coming to my rescue. "His bed is the mostest fun bed there is."

"Yeah," agreed another, "I wish I had one. It's just like a cave."

"Or a fort," another chimed in.

Inspired, I asked, "Lee, would you boys like to show your bed to Susie and the other girls? They've never seen it."

Lee, still ruffled, replied ungraciously, "I guess so. But Susie can't touch it and get girl germs all over it." He shot Susie a triumphant look, intimating that being a girl was far worse than having C/F.

The birthday guests trooped up the stairs, and with trembling hands I started salvaging the melting ice cream. In Lee's room, he and the other boys were explaining the mysteries of the mist tent to a finally-silenced Susie and her friends.

That night, I recounted the day's events to Kay. "I didn't handle it well at all," I concluded, "but it took me so by surprise—and with all his friends around—I didn't know what to say."

"Sounds to me like you handled it okay," he responded. He gave me a squeeze and began to chuckle.

"What are you laughing at?" I demanded.

"Oh, I was just thinking about Lee wanting you to go over and punch Susie's mother's lights out. He's a spunky little kid."

That night I stood quietly by Lee's bed, his form barely discernible through the thick mist in his tent. He was spunky, all right. But inside that spirited body lived a tender little soul, a little boy who gave his mother dandelions in the spring and roses in the fall and who kissed her goodnight and told her that he loved her.

At age 3, Lee graduated from his crib to a regular bed with a mist tent.

—1969—

Lee was most vulnerable to infections during the winter months when the children brought colds and flu home from school. However, by the end of April he had escaped with only two short bouts of pneumonia. With only a month of school remaining and the smell of spring in the air, I thought we were home free.

I should have known better. On the first day of May, he awoke with a burning fever and the deep, strangling cough we had grown to know so well. During the succeeding days, Dr. Venning tried many antibiotics with no measurable success. Coughing racked his body, and he lost weight rapidly. Usually a whirlwind of activity, now he only wanted to be held and rocked.

I was nervous and felt he should be in the hospital, but Dr. Venning disagreed. He said my equipment at home was geared more toward C/F than the hospital's; and, after years of practice, I was more experienced in postural drainage than the nurses, who at that time had little or no training in the procedure.

Lee was still ill on his birthday, but we tried to make it a happy one, and for a few minutes he was caught up in the excitement of blowing out the six candles on his cake and unwrapping his gaily-wrapped present. But soon he tired, and after his drainage he crawled into bed. I adjusted the plastic canopy and clicked on the nebulizer.

I was turning to leave when, without warning, he coughed sharply and choked. Screaming for Kay, I snatched him up, flipped him head down over my lap, and pounded his back. He strained to cough. I pounded harder, and he spewed out a plug of petrified greenish-brown mucus. Coughing and choking, he vomited again and again. Then it was over. Spent and sweaty, he lay cradled in my arms, his breathing uneven, his heart racing.

Kay and the children had come running at my scream. Although Lee had choked for only a few seconds, it frightened us; and now we put our arms around each other, laughing and crying as people do after a terrifying experience.

Hours later, certain that Lee wasn't going to choke again, I crawled into bed. I was just drifting off when I heard a muffled sound from the downstairs bedroom. Quietly, I tiptoed down the stairs. Steve's head was buried beneath his pillow, and he was crying. When I touched him, he sat up and threw his arms around me. Sobs shook his hard, eleven-year-old body. "It's okay," I whispered, stroking his hair. "It's okay."

"I was scared that he was going to choke to death," he cried brokenly.

"I know," I comforted. "He frightened all of us, but he's okay now and sound asleep."

But Steve continued to cry. "Do you want to talk?" I whispered. He nodded, and putting my arm around him, I steered him into the family room. There, curled up in Kay's big leather chair, an afghan tucked around us to ward off the night's chill, I held him in my arms while he poured out the anguish of his little heart. He was not only terrified that Lee would die, but that "something" might happen to Kay and me. If Lee could die, then his mother and father could die, too. What would become of him then?

"Nothing is going to happen to your dad and me," I said, trying to comfort him. "We plan on living a long, long time. By the time we're old and tired and it's time for us to move on, you'll be married with a family of your own. You'll be fine." Then we talked about death being only a temporary separation and that in heaven, we'd be reunited as a family again, and there would be no illness or death to make us sad and afraid.

It was then that Steve shared his deepest torment. Swallowing painfully, he said, "I know all that, but I still don't want Lee to die—not even if he gets real sick and is in lots of pain and he'd be happier in heaven. I can't bear the thought of him leaving us."

I didn't know what to say to comfort him. All I could do was hold him tightly in my arms, my tears mingling with his. Unknowingly, my young son had articulated the feelings buried deep in my own heart. I could not bear the thought of losing Lee either. When the time came, would I have the strength and faith to say, "Thy will be done"? I didn't know.

It was nearly morning before Steve fell asleep, and even then an occasional shudder shook his body. I eased him off my lap and gingerly straightened my cramped legs. Covering him with a blanket, I shut the family room door, hoping he would sleep for an hour before I had to wake him for his paper route.

I didn't go to bed at once. Instead, I stood at the foot of each child's bed, looking into their sleeping faces. I ended up at Lee's bed. He was sleeping peacefully for the first time in weeks. The worst of this bout was over, but I wondered for the hundredth time what effect his illness was having on the other children. Were they, like Steven, each harboring secret fears? It is one thing for children to be aware of family challenges, but quite another to be consumed by them. Kay and I were trying to provide a stable, happy home environment and not let Lee's illness consume us. Were we succeeding? Only time would tell.

In September, Pat joined Mary at Brigham Young University, and Lee started Monroe Elementary School. I don't know who looked forward more to fall—Pat anticipating college, or Lee anticipating first grade.

It didn't matter to Lee that going to school meant getting up by six o'clock every morning to get his treatments done. Each night, he carefully marked another day off the kitchen calendar until finally it was the night before the big event. In spite of my repeated promises to wake him in time, when the kitchen door slammed behind Stan and Steve at 5:00 a.m. as they left on their paper routes, he leaped from his bed, positive that he had been forgotten.

Lee never knew how close he came to not attending school

that first year—not because of ill health, but because of a school nurse!

I had met with his first-grade teacher earlier in the summer, and we had discussed Lee's health. She had taught one of his brothers, and said she was looking forward to having Lee in her class. Thinking we were all set, I was stunned when a few weeks later, the school nurse called and said that Lee couldn't attend school because he had C/F. At first, I thought it was someone's idea of a sick joke. But, incredibly, it was no joke. It truly was the school nurse, and she repeated her statement that Lee couldn't attend school.

I explained that cystic fibrosis was not contagious, and that he would be no threat to his classmates. In fact, the opposite was true. His catching a cold from them would not mean the mere inconvenience of a runny nose and stuffed-up head. It could mean pneumonia and a lengthy hospital stay. Yet it was a risk we had to take in order for him to live a normal life.

She responded crisply that she knew all that. Baffled, I asked, "Well then, why are you saying he can't attend school?"

"You know why," she said, her voice rising. "One day he'll drop dead in class, and it will traumatize the children, that's why!"

"He'll do *what*?" I cried. Surely I hadn't heard her correctly. This was a *nurse* speaking, after all!

But I had heard her correctly. She was convinced that Lee would drop dead in class. Someone she "knew" had "heard" of a child in another state who had done just that, and she wasn't going to let it happen in "her" school district.

I pointed out that several C/F children were attending public schools in Boise as well as schools throughout the state, and their presence in school had not been questioned. The chances of Lee's dropping dead in school were no greater than any other child's. But she didn't budge, and, realizing that she was completely irrational on the point, I gave up trying to be tactful. "I'm sorry you feel that way," I said, "but Lee is going to start school in

September, and you can't prevent him. I want the name of your superior."

"I *can* prevent him," she replied coldly, "and you'll only waste everyone's time going over my head. We're all agreed that your son's attendance at school is not in the best interest of the other children." With that, she hung up the phone.

I was shocked. How could a school nurse keep a child from attending school? And, if she could, how could I tell a child who had nearly worn out his school supplies packing and repacking them that he couldn't go?

The more I thought of it, the angrier I became. The next morning I called Marilee Gross, a long-time acquaintance and a member of the school board. She was as shocked as I was and promised to get back to me. True to her promise, she called back a few days later. After considerable effort, she had convinced the physician who served with the school district to overrule the nurse's decision.

And so it was that on opening day, Lee skipped merrily off to school with his two brothers.

—1970—

Personality-wise, Lee, at seven, was an intriguing mix of his ancestral lines, sometimes displaying the drollness and blarney of his Irish forefathers and other times the dry wit and bulldog tenacity of his English great-grandparents.

His innocent look and slight build belied his enthusiasm for rough play. More than once, he flew through the air trying to block a hard-charging brother. But it didn't faze him; looking astonished that he was the one flat on his back instead of his intended victim, he would blink a few times and then dive head-long into the fray again.

That spring, he entered a one-day, all-city elementary school wrestling tournament. After all the years Stan had practiced wrestling holds on him, he knew he would win. And he did win the first bout, mainly because his ferocious approach so unnerved his opponent that he was pinned before he knew what was hap-pening. Flashing a triumphant grin at Kay and me, he moved cockily on to his second bout.

Swaggering a bit, he used the same threatening stance, but this little boy also had a victory under his belt and was not intimi-dated. They seesawed back and forth, each one making points, but neither able to pin the other.

As the contest wore on, I could see that Lee was becoming short of breath. Sensing victory, the other lad had a rush of adrenalin; and, although Lee escaped being pinned, he lost on points. This time there was no victory swagger as he stalked toward his next adversary.

He managed to hang on and win the third bout on points, but it took everything he had. The fourth bout was no contest; his strength was gone, and he was quickly pinned. Clearly disappointed to be eliminated, he returned to the sidelines without a glance in our direction.

However, by the time he'd wolfed down two hamburgers and a milk shake on the way home, his self-esteem was back, and he was chortling happily over his two victories, explaining with relish each hold used to accomplish the feat.

Macho exterior notwithstanding, Lee was a loving boy, and for Mother's Day he made me a special card. Beneath painstakingly-drawn flowers he printed, "Mothers are fine! Mothers are kind! I hope my mother stays fine and kind!" Then, in cramped handwriting near the bottom, he added, "I'm small enough to be hugged and kissed still."

In July, Lee attended his first C/F camp. Early in the summer, Miriam E. Breidenstein, the Seattle Children's Orthopedic Hospital Camp Coordinator, invited him to a five-day camp at the Sunset Lake Youth Camp in Washington. She would meet him and my friend Lu Goold's C/F daughter, Cindy, at the Seattle airport and take them to her home for the night. They would go on to camp the next morning. As head of the Pulmonary-Cardiac Department, she had already made arrangements to borrow inhalation equipment and mist tents from the hospital, and she would administer their treatments herself.

We readily accepted her generous offer. Lee excitedly packed and unpacked his bag every day for weeks, boasting happily that he would catch "the biggest fish ever" and bring it home for me to cook.

As I watched Lee's excitement mount, I thought how crushed he'd be if an infection flared at the last minute and he couldn't go. Surreptitiously, I scrutinized him each day for warning signs, ready to rush him to Dr. Venning's office at the slightest hint of trouble. But his health held, and we trooped to the airport to see him off. I thought he might have some last-minute misgivings, but as I leaned over to kiss him goodbye, his eyes were sparkling with anticipation. Mr. Confidence himself, he grinned up at me, dimples flashing in his cheeks. Dwarfed by the high-backed airplane seat, he looked very much the little boy that he was. Sensing my concern, Cindy, eleven now and on her third trip to camp, patted my hand and said in a motherly tone, "Don't you worry, Mrs. Belnap. I'll take good care of him." I didn't doubt her word for a minute.

The first day he was gone, I wandered around the house not knowing what to do with myself. There were no treatments to give, no equipment to scrub and disinfect, no trips to the doctor. However, once I started canning and sewing, the days flew by, and soon it was time to meet our little camper at the airport.

What a shock that was! Instead of the squeaky-clean little boy in freshly ironed pants and starched shirt who boarded the plane, there emerged a dirty-faced little urchin in an incredibly filthy shirt, the tail of which hung half in, half out of equally filthy pants. A huge safety pin held a gaping rip together at the knee. Had it not been for the dancing hazel eyes and the big grin that split his face, we would never have recognized him.

Spying us, he broke into a run and hurled himself into my arms. Holding my breath against the worst stench I'd smelled in my life, I caught him up and gave him a big kiss. The dreadful odor was explained when he reached into a paper bag and proudly hauled out a small, very ripe fish. "See," he proclaimed triumphantly, "I told you I'd catch a fish for dinner, and I did!"

Lee had not only enjoyed a fabulous five days, his first ever away from his family, but he had also become aware of some of the physical problems of other children, one of whom was a boy about his age who had hemophilia. In telling us about him, he said, "He had to sit in a wheelchair all the time because just before camp he'd bumped his knee, and it was all swelled up. The counselor told us we could talk to him, but we had to stay back from him and his wheelchair because if we bumped him he would bleed inside and have to go back home and be put in the hospital. I talked to him lots, and we played some word games together. He was real good and beat me every time. I'm sure glad I have C/F and not what he has. I'd hate not being able to play."

Mostly, however, he talked about his friend, Bobby*, a C/F boy about his own age. Listening, I hoped he was exaggerating their exploits, because if he weren't, I doubted if either of them would be invited back to camp!

In the meantime, the maturing of our older children was beginning to bring about significant changes in our family. Mary, home for the summer from BYU, met and began dating a young man named Dee Cazier. Three days after Christmas, she married him in the Logan LDS temple.

All of us were going to miss her, but it was especially hard for Lee. He sat on the edge of her bed and somberly watched her pack. Catching the glint of tears in his eyes, Mary left her packing and knelt down in front of him. Tipping his chin up so she could look into his eyes, she said, "It's okay, Lee. It doesn't matter that we won't be sharing the same room any longer; we'll still be sharing each other's hearts."

---

*Name changed.

—1971—

New Year's morning Lee awakened with a hoarse cough, and I wondered uneasily if I should call Dr. Venning. I decided not to. Except for the cough, he seemed fine, and I was reluctant to disturb the doctor on a holiday.

By evening he had a slight fever and headache, but his color was good and he was breathing easily. Shortly after midnight, however, his condition deteriorated. His temperature shot up to 104.6, and his limbs jerked as if manipulated by a puppeteer. He was dangerously close to having a convulsion. I hurriedly filled a basin with tepid water, and while Kay draped cool towels on him, I ran downstairs to phone Dr. Venning.

There was no dial tone! It had stormed all evening, and the icy snow had broken a phone line. The electric power lines had escaped, but the phone was useless. I tore back up the stairs. "The phone's out, and I can't get through," I cried. "Is he any better?" I knew his condition couldn't have changed in the few seconds I'd been away, but I had to ask anyway.

Hearing my voice, Lee's eyelids fluttered open, revealing glassy eyes. His abdomen heaved, flattening out against his spine in a wheezing effort to suck oxygen into laboring lungs. His face was a dirty blue-gray.

Kay gave him a blessing, and he seemed a little better. I walked to the opposite side of the room and motioned for Kay to follow me. "I think we can get him to the hospital now without risking a convulsion," I said, my voice unsteady in spite of my attempt to speak calmly.

Kay rubbed a peephole on the frosted windowpane and peered into the darkness. "It looks like it's stopped snowing," he said, "but it would still take at least three-quarters of an hour on these roads to make it. That's a long time for him to be without mist when he's having so much trouble breathing. I think he's better off here, at least until his breathing improves."

"But what if it gets worse instead of better?" I whispered through stiff lips. "He needs to be in the hospital where they can give him oxygen or do an emergency tracheotomy or something. We're helpless here." My voice broke, and I turned away.

Kay put his arm around me. "Let's give him ten more minutes," he advised. "Then if he looks like he's getting worse, we'll take our chances and make a run for it. But for now, I think he's better off here."

Reluctantly, I agreed. My brain knew Kay was right, but every fiber of my being cried out for action. Doing something, even if it were the wrong thing, seemed preferable to doing nothing. I tried the phone again. Still no dial tone.

Ten minutes passed. He was no better, but no worse either. Another ten minutes, and then another ten. We kept sponging his hot little body. As minutes stretched into hours, ever so gradually his breathing became less labored, and the croupy coughing spasms became less frequent. His temperature came down to 103.2, and he fell into a troubled sleep. I suggested to Kay that he rest. I would watch Lee.

Switching off all the lights except a night light, I pulled a chair close to his bed and tucked a blanket around my legs. Groping under the heavy plastic, I found his hand; his fingers closed around mine. His wheezing was even more pronounced in the stillness of the night, and I longed for morning to come.

At last, I heard Stan's alarm, followed by the banging of sliding closet doors downstairs. It was 5:00 a.m., and Stan and Steve were putting on their heavy winter gear, preparing to deliver papers. It was morning.

It was nearly seven o'clock before the phone lines were repaired. I had never called Dr. Venning that early in the morning before; but once I heard the dial tone, I didn't hesitate a second. Quickly, I apprised him of the night's happenings and asked if he would meet me at the hospital. He hesitated, then said to meet him at his office instead. With the hospital across the street, it would take only minutes to admit him.

While Kay warmed up the car, I bundled Lee up for the trip across town. One of us needed to be at home, and Kay knew that I'd go crazy if it were me; so he kept to himself whatever concerns he felt about me driving the snow-filled roads alone, saying only, "Drive carefully," before giving me a quick kiss and slamming the car door shut.

I cautiously nosed the car into the pre-dawn darkness shrouding the city. The snowplows and sanding trucks had not yet reached the outskirts of the city; I gripped the steering wheel tightly, struggling to keep the chained tires in the tracks made by a previous traveler, fearful that at any second the car would slide and mire down in the drifted snow. Except for my headlights probing the street ahead, everything was dark. Snow muffled the usual sounds of a stirring city, and only Lee's raspy breathing and the crunch of tires on the frozen snow broke the unnatural quiet. Feeling isolated, I wondered uneasily if heading out by myself had been such a good idea. Suppose I got stuck? What then?

As if in response to my fears, the back end of the car slid toward the side of the road, and I knew I was only inches away from becoming hopelessly stuck. Turning the wheel into the slide, I prayed the back tires would grab the surface before I ran out of maneuvering room. Miraculously, they did. The car straightened, and I eased it back into the frozen tracks, my heart pounding.

At last, the welcome red of a stop light signaled my entry into the downtown grid. Here the streets were sanded, and soon I was driving past the brightly-lit hospital and turning into Dr. Venning's parking lot. For the first time, it occurred to me that the doctor, too, might be having problems with the slick roads, and I was relieved when I saw that the clinic's lights were on. He was waiting for us and would know what to do.

Lee had willingly let Kay carry him to the car, but when I

leaned over to pick him up, he pushed my arms aside and croaked, "I'm not a baby. I can walk." As we made our way into the office, the first snowflakes of still another winter storm began to fall.

Dr. Venning had to pause several times during his examination for Lee's coughing to subside; but finally he rose from his three-legged stool and grunted, "There's so much noise in his lungs that I won't know exactly what we're up against until I get an x-ray and some blood work. About all I know now is that he has diffused bronchitis. His temperature is down from what you said it was during the night, but it's still over 103. That may or may not be significant." He glanced at his watch. "The hospital lab doesn't open this early on Saturdays, but I'll phone and see if someone's there who can make certain he's the first one in when they do open."

Picking up his stool, he headed toward his office, his steps echoing in the deserted building. Abruptly, he halted and came back to the examining room. Gripping Lee's shoulder, he said, "Don't worry, boy, you're going to be all right." Those words, accompanied by a grip on the shoulder, had become a ritual between the doctor and his small patient over the years. Lee grinned weakly, and promptly went into another exhausting round of coughing. Dr. Venning hurried off to call the lab.

The x-rays and blood work completed, Lee and I made our way back to Dr. Venning's office. The clinic was now in full swing, with babies crying and nurses hurrying from room to room. We waited anxiously in the doctor's private office for him to bring us the results of the tests. We didn't have long to wait.

Feeling for Lee's pulse, he grunted, "His x-ray is unremarkable. Naturally, his white count and sed rate are high, but I expected that." He listened to Lee's lungs again, and then sat down at his desk. Fishing antibiotic samples out of a drawer, he handed them to me, saying, "I'll write out a prescription for polycillin; but in the meantime, start him on these."

"Aren't you going to hospitalize him?" I gasped, unnerved at the thought of spending another night like the one we'd just been through.

He looked surprised. "No need to," he replied. "He has bronchitis, and with such a high temperature, probably a virus. He'll sound tight and wheezy for the next few days, but he's over the worst of it. Call me tomorrow afternoon at home, and then bring him into the office on Monday." With that, he dismissed us.

Lee improved each day, and the following week, the doctor gave him the green light to go back to school. In one week's time, he had gone from fighting to breathe to fighting with his brothers. Incredible.

Lee hadn't mentioned Bobby, his best friend at the previous year's camp, for several months, and I thought he had forgotten him. However, as July neared and Mrs. Breidenstein again opened her heart and home to Lee and Cindy, his name entered into almost all of his conversations. He could scarcely wait to see him.

Once more, the Belnap and Goold families assembled at the airport to see their campers off to Seattle. Cindy was very much into the "big sister" role and hovered over Lee incessantly—something I appreciated, but which caused him to roll his eyes. A week later, we were back at the airport, eyes searching the passengers as they walked down the ramp. Recalling the fish episode of the prior year, I fervently hoped he wasn't bringing me his "catch" again. Then, there he was! He let out a yell and hurled himself down the ramp and into our arms.

In the midst of the noisy welcome, Cindy tugged at my elbow and drew me aside. "Don't ask him about Bobby," she whispered. "He wasn't to camp this year, so he's probably dead." I froze, not knowing what to say. What made Cindy think Bobby had died simply because he wasn't at camp? There could be a hundred other reasons.

"Maybe he was on vacation with his folks or something. Did someone tell you he'd died?" I asked, finding my tongue at last.

"No, but I overheard Lee ask his counselor where he was, and the counselor said he wouldn't be coming to camp anymore. When the counselors say someone won't be coming back to camp and don't give the reason, that means they're dead," she said patiently, sounding like an adult explaining something to a backward child. "Lee doesn't know that meant Bobby died," she continued. "He's too little to figure things out yet; but next year he'll probably catch on that it's better not to ask why someone's not there. That way, you can pretend they're still alive."

I looked at this little wisp of a girl, barely twelve years old. Already touched by death, she wanted to protect her little friend's innocence for at least another year. My eyes misted over, and I gave her a little squeeze. "I won't ask about Bobby," I promised.

In the fall, Lee started the third grade, and Irene joined Pat at Brigham Young University. With Mary married, I was now living in an all-male family. How I missed my daughters!

Lee, age 10, having fun on the lake at McCall.

— 1972 —

Lee contracted a stubborn case of pneumonia in April, and he was still fighting it on his ninth birthday in May. Nevertheless, the day began on a bright note, with Dr. Venning's nurses sneaking treats to him and wishing him a happy birthday. Unfortunately, his day deteriorated shortly after that.

Dr. Venning listened to his lungs, and then, as he'd done twice a week for the past three weeks, he sent us to the hospital for a blood test and x-ray. After we returned to the clinic, Lee busied himself with homework while we waited for the test results. When the doctor came in, he was frowning. He told Lee to stay put and motioned for me to follow him to his office. Once there, he said brusquely, "Lee has pseudomonas aeruginosa pneumonia."

My heart sank. Pseudomonas aeruginosa was a much-feared bacteria that often colonized in the lungs of C/F patients. It had the uncanny ability to sense danger and generated a slimy carbohydrate sac that prevented penetration by antibiotics, making it virtually immune to them.

"He's in trouble," the doctor continued grimly. "Today's x-ray shows the pneumonia is infiltrating new areas, and his sed rate and white count are skyrocketing. I'm going to start him on a new antibiotic called gentamicin. It has to be administered by shot, and will need to be given every eight hours for at least ten days." He looked at his watch. "It's nearly 3:00. I'll have Dortha give him his first shot, and then you'll need to give him one every eight hours at home."

"Me, give him a shot?" I echoed mindlessly.

He looked surprised. "You give shots, don't you?"

I shook my head, not volunteering that I had this "thing"

about needles and shots. Even holding my babies while they received their immunizations made me light-headed and nauseous. "I'm not a nurse," I reminded him.

"Oh, I forgot. I always think of you as one." He sounded disappointed, and I felt I'd let him down. "Well, then, unless you know a nurse who'll come to your home, we'll have to hospitalize him," he concluded reluctantly.

I thought of Annie Cannon, a retired nurse in our ward. I disliked asking her for such a huge favor, but I disliked the idea of hospitalizing Lee even more.

While Dortha prepared the shot, we walked back to the examining room. Once more Lee breathed deeply through his mouth while Dr. Venning listened to his lungs. Each breath triggered a violent coughing attack. Removing the stethoscope from his ears, the doctor stepped back and spoke directly to his patient. "Son, you've got a stubborn bug in there called pseudomonas. Dortha is going to give you a shot before you leave, and you'll have to have three a day for the next ten days. The shots will burn and make your butt sore, but you can handle it."

Lee had only one question. "I can still go to school, can't I?"

Regardless of how ill he was, he seldom missed school. Dr. Venning looked at the pale face with its dark circles and started to shake his head. Then he caught the plea in Lee's voice and changed his mind. "If you let your mother take you to and from school in the car and stay in your room during play time, you can go," he agreed. Lee smiled his thanks.

Annie arrived promptly at 11:00 p.m. that night and gave him his shot. Hearing Lee's quick intake of breath as the medicine burned into his thigh, I felt sick. What a lousy way to end a birthday.

For the next two days, Annie cheerfully gave Lee shots three times a day with never a hint that it was an imposition. However, by the end of the second day, I knew it was time to put my childish phobia aside, and I asked her to teach me to give shots. We practiced on a grapefruit. Even poking the needle through its skin made me sick, but that night I gave Lee the first of thousands of shots I would give him over the ensuing years. True, I threw up immediately afterward, but at least I didn't pass out.

The ten days of shots ended up being sixteen days. Before they were over, Lee's buttocks were so sore that he shuffled like an old man when he walked, and negotiating the stairs to his room was excruciating. Leaning heavily on the rail, he eased himself up one painful step at a time. Often I saw tears in his eyes, but he didn't cry. I would have felt better if he had. Somehow, through it all, he hung on to his sense of humor. Once, when Dr. Venning asked him about his mother's expertise, he grinned and said, "Let's put it this way. She takes aim, closes her eyes, and hurls the needle like a dart. It was pretty funny the time she stuck herself instead of me." Luckily, Dr. Venning assumed he was joking.

On June 14, we buried my mother. Nursing my own grief, I hadn't realized how Lee had been affected by her death until weeks later when he crawled into my lap and asked, "What do you think Grandma's doing right now?"

"I don't know," I answered, "but I suspect she's making someone happy—that's what she liked doing the most."

"I'll bet she's making a pie," he announced confidently. "Whenever she visited us, she always made pies. Remember how she rolled the pieces of left-over crust together and put cinnamon and sugar on top and baked them for me?"

I nodded my head.

He was silent for a minute and then asked, "Do you think she's lonely and misses us?"

"I think she misses us, but I think it's in a different way than the way we miss her. As for being lonely, I don't think so. She's with your Grandpa Smith and her mom and dad and brothers and sisters, to say nothing of all her other relatives and friends."

At that, he burst into tears and buried his face in my neck. "But what if she can't find them?" he cried. "Heaven must be a long way off, and what if it's dark and she's scared?"

It was then that I realized that his concerns were not just for his grandmother. They were also a little boy's fears of death. I held him close and stroked his hair. "Honey," I asked, "are you afraid you'll die and be all alone?" He nodded and continued to weep. For a few seconds I sat there, holding him, praying that the right words would come. Then, as if it had happened only yesterday, I remembered.

"Lee, I was about your age when my grandmother died. For a long time afterward, I couldn't sleep at night because I thought I might die, too, and I was afraid I'd get lost trying to find my way back to Heavenly Father. Sometimes, just thinking about it scared me so much that I'd crawl in bed with my mother and dad."

Lee sat bolt upright in shock, tears forgotten. "I'd never do anything sissy like that," he exclaimed. "But then, of course, I'm not a girl."

"Of course not," I murmured. "Anyway, one night my mother held me on her lap just like I'm holding you, and she explained that Heavenly Father knows where each of us is every minute. We're never lost to Him—not when we're born into this world, not while we live here, and not when we leave it. Actually, dying is much like being born, only this time instead of leaving Heavenly Father to come here, we leave here and return to Him."

"But dying is scarier than being born," he interrupted. "Susie said that when you die, you're all alone in the dark."

Our old nemesis, Susie, again! "Nonsense," I said briskly. "Susie's wrong. Heaven is a radiant, beautiful place. As for being alone, that's silly. When you were born, Heavenly Father didn't just dump you down here with no warning and with no one to care for you, now did he? Of course not! Daddy and I knew for months you were coming to live with us, and the instant you left your Heavenly Father's arms, you came into ours. When you die, your dad and I will be waiting in heaven for you, just like we waited for you here before you were born."

"But what if I die first? Then I'll be all alone," he argued, still afraid.

Holding him tight, I answered, "Lee, I don't expect you to die first; but if you do, someone will be waiting for you. And, knowing how much your grandma loves you, I'll bet Heavenly Father would let her be the one."

"But what if she's late, and I'm all by myself until she gets there? Sometimes she was late, you know. Not very often," he admitted, "but once in a while."

Gently, I tilted his head back so that I could look into his anxious eyes. "Lee, I promise that you will never be alone, not for a second. If your Heavenly Father calls you home first, your dad and I will hold you in our arms until someone you love comes for you. You will never be alone."

We sat quietly for a long time. The tension slowly drained from his little body, and for the first time since he was a toddler, he fell asleep in my arms. Looking down at his tear-smudged face, I wondered if my simplified version of life after death had stilled his fears as my mother's once had mine.

Early that fall my friend, Lu Goold, called. She had just returned from the University of Utah Medical Center where Cindy had been hospitalized. I was stunned by her message. The Salt Lake C/F Clinic had discontinued the use of mist tents. They thought the mist was doing more harm than good! For nine years I'd been told that mist was an absolute must for C/F children. Now I was being told that it was making them worse. I immediately called Dr. Eugene Brown, the Director of the Idaho C/F Clinic; and, like me, he was also shocked. However, he was going to continue with mist therapy until he was officially told otherwise. In the meantime, I could do whatever I felt was best for Lee.

We had an appointment with Dr. Venning that afternoon, and I told him what Lu had said. Recalling his initial qualms about mist tents, I thought he would be in total agreement with the clinic's decision. Instead he said, "Originally, I had misgivings about using mist, but I think now that it may have given Lee the edge he needed to make it through some critical times, especially as an infant. Of course," he added, leaning over Lee, "there have always been risks associated with mist tents, and perhaps that's why Salt Lake has discontinued them." I waited for him to continue, but he busied himself with his patient, telling him to breathe deeply while he listened to his lungs. Was that all he was going to say?

Finally I broke the silence. "What about Lee?" I asked. "Do we ignore the clinic's recommendation and leave him in, or do we take him out?"

He shrugged. "Personally, I don't think the mist tent is doing him any harm; but now that he's older, it may not be doing him any good, either. If you'd feel more comfortable taking him out, it's fine with me."

"If I'd feel more comfortable!" I wasn't going to feel comfortable either way if I was forced to make the decision. Wasn't that what doctors were supposed to do?

Dr. Venning continued to study Lee's lab reports. His white count, when he was well, was between 8,000 and 10,000. Now it was 21,800, and his sed rate had climbed from ten to twenty-eight. He had pseudomonas pneumonia again. Dr. Venning swore under his breath and ordered gentamicin shots.

In spite of the shots, Lee's white count and sed rate continued to climb, and the pneumonia continued to infiltrate new areas in his lungs. Each time I switched on the nebulizer, I agonized. Was the mist helping him survive the pneumonia, or was it causing it? Kay was out of town, and when I finally reached him, he, too, left the decision to me.

I continued to vacillate—and to pray. Finally, I decided to call Dr. Docter in Seattle. I had thought of calling him before, but had shrugged it off, fearing that he, too, would leave the decision up to me. Now I felt impressed to make the call.

Instead of immediately answering my question, he asked me what Dr. Venning advised. My heart sank. Was the impression to call simply wishful thinking on my part? "He said it was up to me," I answered, sick with disappointment. "But I'm not knowledgeable enough to make that kind of a medical decision, and I don't think I should have to." My voice rose. "What I want is an unequivocal 'yes' or 'no' from a C/F specialist, and you're a C/F specialist. What do you want me to do?"

There was a surprised pause on the other end of the line, and then came the firm reply, "Take him out. Except under special circumstances, we are discontinuing mist tent therapy in our center here."

Following my call to Dr. Docter, Lee and I dismantled the tent. After disinfecting everything for the final time, we packed the equipment into boxes and put it on a high shelf in the back of his closet. Then we remade his bed with regular sheets and quilts. That night, we stared at each other blankly. There was no plastic canopy to arrange, no equipment to turn on, no hissing of nebulizers or swirling of mist. Just a nine-year-old boy lying in an ordinary bed, like countless other nine-year-old boys throughout the city.

Halloween evening, Lee, dressed in a pirate's costume, an earring dangling from one ear and charcoal smudges on his face, raced off with his friends to "Trick or Treat" on our street. Briefly, I questioned my sanity. This was the first day he'd been off shots in three weeks, and it was cold outside. When he returned an hour later, however, his animated face told me I'd made the correct decision. Occasionally, good sense has to be ignored, and on that particular night having fun proved as healing to Lee's spirit as the antibiotics had been to his body. He had needed both.

On November 20, the second of our children was married. Pat married Robert Johnson in the Salt Lake Temple. They would make their home in Spanish Fork while she finished her schooling at BYU. She was a radiant bride, but even while I rejoiced in her happiness, I felt a tug at my heartstrings as another of my daughters left home to begin a new life.

—1973—

In March, Cindy Goold passed away. She was thirteen. We didn't encourage Lee to visit her when she came home from the hospital for the last time. We wanted him to remember her as the solicitous little "mother" with the big smile and bright eyes who had hovered over him at camp, not as she looked when Kay and I saw her shortly before she died.

Lee turned ten in May. His once blond hair was dark now, but his dimples still flashed when he smiled, and his hazel eyes continued to reflect his moods, solemn one moment, merry the next. Although he ate enormous amounts of food, he was thin. I could almost span his waist with my hands, but his shoulders were broad like his father's, making him appear heavier than he actually was.

He had many friends, most of whom had grown up with him. They were as accepting of his way of life as he was, and often our family room overflowed with boisterous little boys waiting for Lee to finish his treatments. Once finished, off they ran to do those exciting, wonderful things that ten-year-old boys do.

Young as he was, Lee loved sports, and he played them year round. Instead of fall, winter, and spring, his seasons were football, basketball, and baseball. He was never the best player on his team; in fact, I would say he was about average. But occasionally he was the hero—like the time his baseball team was one run behind in the bottom of the last inning with a runner on second with two outs and Lee up to bat. He trotted to the plate, and the coach of the opposing team motioned his outfield to move in. I knew he figured this little kid for a sure out. The game was in the bag.

If Lee was concerned, he gave no indication. He made a few practice swings and then crouched into his hitting stance. The pitcher narrowed his eyes, wound up, and threw a strike directly over the plate. Lee swung, and the ball cracked off his bat in a solid hit, flying high over the heads of the fielders. Shocked, everyone froze except Lee. The instant the ball left his bat, he was off, legs churning around the bases, going for broke. As he neared home, the relay player threw hard to his crouching catcher. Lee's coach screamed, "Slide, slide," and Lee threw his body head first toward the plate in the longest, most unorthodox slide I've ever seen, beating the tag by a fingertip.

His teammates rushed to his side, and for a few moments I thought they were going to pummel him to death; but he emerged unscathed, completely winded, and grinning from ear to ear. I don't know where he found the breath to run those bases, but run them he most certainly did; and that night during his treatment, he recounted his heroics over and over again to his appreciative father.

By December, however, it was difficult to believe that this was the same boy who had slid so triumphantly into home plate. His clothes hung on him, and his face was white and drawn. He coughed incessantly, and at night he sat hunched forward, his forearms resting on his knees in order to breathe. He'd been on gentamicin shots for weeks, and the pneumonia was still spreading. I was frightened, and Dr. Venning looked more concerned with each visit; but Lee was positive he'd be well for Christmas. That was his favorite time of year, and he had no intention of having it ruined with shots. After all, Christmas was about believing, wasn't it? All we had to do was believe hard enough.

As day followed day with no visible improvement, I alternated between faith and fear—faith that a little boy's prayers would be answered, and fear that he would be disappointed. In the end, his faith proved strong enough for both of us, and three days before Christmas he started to improve. On the afternoon of Christmas Eve, Dr. Venning clapped him on the back and said, "No more shots, boy. We've turned it around. You're going to be okay." Lee shot me an "I told you so" look, and wished his doctor and nurses a Merry Christmas. He was ready for Christmas Eve to begin.

By the time we arrived home, Christmas lights had already transformed our neighborhood into a sparkling fairyland, and soon the spirit of Christmas permeated our home. Smothered whispers and delighted giggles issued from behind closed doors, and unseen hands stealthily slipped beribboned gifts beneath the tree. The spicy aroma of a steaming Christmas carrot pudding drifted from the kitchen, and Christmas carols played softly in the background. Kay read St. Luke's account of the birth of the Savior, and afterward the children hung their Christmas stockings from the mantle and set out cookies and milk for Santa's midnight snack.

Our long wait in the doctor's office that afternoon had put me behind in my baking. As soon as everyone was in bed, I took out my mixing bowls, turned the radio to some soft Christmas music, and started making preparations for the next day's Christmas dinner. It was late when I finished; and, rubbing my tired back, I walked into the living room and clicked off the Christmas tree lights. Standing at the window, I drank in the winter scene. In the middle of the yard, a snow fort guarded a lopsided snowman. I smiled, happy that I still had boys young enough to build forts and snowmen. My smile faded a bit, however, as I recalled Lee's wistful face pressed against the window, watching his brothers building them. Cutting snowmen out of cookie dough with Irene was fun, but not as much fun as building real ones with his brothers.

As if my thoughts had conjured him up, he appeared at the top of the stairs.

"Too excited to sleep?" I asked.

"Naw. I keep coughing, so I thought I might as well get up and bug you. But I see I'm too late—you're headed for bed."

I glanced at my watch. "I'm not tired," I lied, "and it won't be long until it's officially Christmas. Shall we watch it come in together?"

He eyed me speculatively and asked, "Does that mean I can open my presents as soon as it's midnight?"

"No, but if you're hungry, we can share Santa's midnight snack."

I switched the Christmas tree lights back on, and he hustled into the kitchen for Santa's treat. With the furnace turned down for the night, the house was chilly; we threw an afghan over us and snuggled companionably in the corner of the sofa, happily munching Christmas cookies and drinking milk.

Across the street, Christmas lights blinked on and off, creating friendly patterns on the snow. In a darkened house further down, a light clicked on. "Bet they forgot to wrap a present," Lee commented.

"Or maybe the children just fell asleep, and Santa had to wait to fill the stockings," I ventured.

Cookies and milk devoured, Lee relaxed against me, and we sat buried in our own thoughts. After a long time, he whispered, "There's a special peacefulness about tonight, isn't there, Mom? Everything's so quiet, almost like the whole world is waiting for Jesus to be born."

Downstairs, the clock chimed midnight. It was Christmas.

Lee's fifth grade school photo.

—1974—

In the fall, Lee signed up for Optimist football. Unfortunately, the coach was a frustrated ex-jock who treated the boys like they were professionals training for the Super Bowl rather than eleven- and twelve-year-old kids. It was bad enough that the practices were long and brutal, but the killer was the laps he required the boys to run when they were already exhausted from practice. Even the strongest boys had problems with that, and several boys quit the team.

For Lee, the laps were unbelievably punishing. Every evening he returned home white and trembling with fatigue, but when I urged him to quit he wouldn't hear of it. He said that he only needed to toughen up, and he'd be fine. He did, however, condescend to being chauffeured to and from his practices, eliminating the mile-long bike ride.

When I arrived at the field early one evening, I was sickened by what I saw. Lagging far behind the others, Lee was fighting for breath, his face twisted with pain. Even as I watched, he staggered and fell to his hands and knees. For a moment he rested on all fours, head hanging down between his arms. Then he forced his body up, stumbled a few more steps, and fell heavily on the cinders. His coach yelled at him to get up and "be a man".

Over Lee's objections, I called his coach that night. I knew that he was aware that Lee had C/F, but I thought he might not know the toll it had taken on his lungs. I stressed that Lee could certainly practice, but that running laps afterward was too much strain on his heart and lungs. I added that Lee would rather the boys on the team not be told that he had C/F.

During dinner the next night, Lee was tense and short with us. During his treatment I found out why. "I told you not to call my coach," he said angrily. "Today at practice, he yelled for everyone to run laps except Belnap. All the kids looked at me and wondered why I didn't have to. Now they think I'm the coach's pet or something," he charged miserably. "You should have stayed out of it. I was doing okay."

The following night when he stepped through the kitchen door, his tear-stained face froze the inquiry about football practice on my lips.

"Are you all right?" I cried, reaching for him.

"I'm all right," he answered curtly. Pushing past me, he hurried up the stairs and into his room, slamming the door behind him.

Giving him time to pull himself together, I finished the casserole I was preparing and put it in the oven. When I entered his room, he was lying face down on his bed. Unconsciously, I cupped my hands and clapped his upper back. Talking always seemed easier when I was giving him a treatment. Even so, neither of us spoke for a long time.

Finally, he said, "I quit football."

I waited for an explanation. When none came, I ventured, "You don't like it anymore?"

"I love it. I don't get to play much, but when I do it's fun." Then he added for my benefit, "And playing in a game doesn't tire me out or make me cough a lot or anything."

"Then why . . . ?"

"Because I can't keep up with the other kids during practices. We do so many drills that by the time we're ready to scrimmage, I'm too out of breath to play good. Then the coach yells at me for being slow."

"Maybe I could call him and—"

"Don't you dare!" he yelled, jumping up and facing me angrily. "You did that last time, and it made things worse. I've quit. Just let it alone." Rushing past me, he stormed across the hall and into the bathroom. The lock clicked, and soon water ran noisily in the tub, covering the sound of crying.

During his treatment that evening, he didn't speak until we were doing the last position. Then he said, "This is the first time I've quit something because of C/F, isn't it?"

I nodded, not knowing what to say. Finally, I ventured, "You know, Lee, lots of boys don't play football, or any sport, for that matter. There are lots of interesting things you can get into besides sports." I knew my words were falling on deaf ears, but I didn't know what else to say.

Later that night, Steve went into Lee's room and stayed for a long time. The next morning, Lee was remarkably cheerful. The reason became evident when he confided, "Steve said that Optimist football is lots tougher than football in junior high. He told me to wait a couple of years until I get to South, and then go out for lightweight. In the meantime, he's going to throw passes to me so I'll be a good receiver when I get there."

So much for my philosophical approach! Eleven-year-old boys bent on playing sports want solutions, not platitudes.

In September, Stan left for London, England, to serve a two-year LDS mission. He had never been away from home before, and England seemed dreadfully far away. I gave him a final hug and kiss, wishing I could turn back the clock and he could be my little boy for a few more years.

When they parted, Lee tried to act nonchalant, but he couldn't quite carry it off, and his eyes filled when Stan took him in his arms for a hard goodbye hug. Over his head, Stan's eyes met mine and clouded over. I knew he was thinking of the difficult conversation of the night before when he'd voiced his fears to his father and me that "something" might happen to Lee while he was gone.

A final squeeze for me, a handshake for his dad, and he walked quickly away without looking back. He left as a boy; he would return as a young man.

—1975—

Lee made it through the winter months well, but late in March a searing pain in his chest jolted him awake. Pain notwithstanding, he insisted on going to school. His class was finishing a project, and he wanted to be in on its final touches. When I objected, he answered irritably, "Mom, I'm fine. It's just a touch of pleurisy or a muscle cramp or something. Anyway, it's not all that bad. Don't make such a big deal of every little thing!" In spite of his words, I knew he was hurting. His face was pale, and he was taking the smallest possible breaths. We ended up compromising. He would go to school that morning and to the doctor in the afternoon.

Promptly at noon, I was at the school. Watching him walk to the car, I was appalled at the change four hours had wrought. His face was a sickly blue-gray, and he was obviously in great pain. I ran around and opened the car door. Hugging his right arm to his chest, he slid carefully into the seat, leaned his head back, and grunted through gritted teeth, "I was dumb to go to school."

"I was dumb to let you," I replied.

Lee and I were with Dr. Venning in his private office when he received the call from the hospital x-ray technician. His diagnosis was a plugged area in the right lung.

Pursing his lips, Dr. Venning drummed his long fingers on his desk and thoughtfully observed Lee, who was doubled forward in pain. His nail beds were dusky, and his lips had a bluish tinge. Without speaking, the doctor rose, walked around the desk, and listened again to Lee's chest, concentrating on the right lobe. Turning to me, he said, "I don't agree that this is a plug. I think he has a collapsed lung, and he needs to be on the next plane to the University of Utah Medical Center. Use the phone in the other office to call the airlines while I call the hospital. I stared at him, wanting to ask questions, but he was already dialing Salt Lake. Waving his hand for me to hurry, he added, "When you talk to the airline, don't volunteer anything about a medical problem. They may not let him aboard if they know he has a collapsed lung. They have oxygen on the plane if he runs into trouble."

The next hour was a blur of activity. At Lee's insistence, I dashed into the school and picked up his books and assignments. I called a neighbor for a ride to the airport, then canceled it when Kay drove into the driveway after being out of town for three days. I packed our suitcases, made out children's schedules, canceled appointments, and called Pat and Robert to meet us at the airport. We could, of course, catch a cab to the hospital, but I felt the need to have family waiting for us at the other end.

I choked up while talking to Pat, and before I could brush away the tears, Lee walked into the room. "You're crying," he accused, alarm spreading across his face. He had never seen me cry before. He looked frightened. "What's the matter?" he demanded. "Dr. Venning said I was going to be okay, and I feel better since he gave me the pain pill. I'm going to be okay, aren't I?"

I gave him a squeeze. "You're going to be fine," I assured him, attempting a smile. "Your mom is just being silly. Mothers do that sometimes."

Kay and a friend gave Lee a blessing, and a few minutes later we were in the air, Lee resting quietly beside me. The codeine had taken the edge off his pain.

C/F patients were housed in the pediatric section on the fifth floor of the hospital, and the first night Lee shared a room with a non-C/F child who was recovering from surgery. However, the following morning he was moved down the hall to Robbie's* room. Robbie was a little C/F boy about seven or eight years old, and he was obviously near respiratory failure. Dwarfed by the monitors and equipment surrounding his bed, he lay doubled

---

*Name changed.

forward on pillows. He was connected to an Intermittent Positive Pressure Machine that forced air into his lungs, and his mother stood over him, ministering to him like a tireless robot. With machine-like precision, she clapped the IPPM mask over his nose and mouth, left it for a few seconds, and then removed it and pushed hard on his chest to force the air out. Mask on, mask off, push. Mask on, mask off, push. Every few minutes she interrupted the routine to pound sharply on his back, trying to dislodge the mucus that was filling his lungs. During those few seconds, Robbie fought to grab the breath-giving mask, terrified eyes reflecting his panic. "You've got to cough, Robbie," she'd say. "After you cough, you can have it back; but you must cough first." Robbie, face purple with effort, would finally manage a strangling cough, and his mother would clap the mask back on his face. Then the cycle would repeat itself.

I jerked the curtain shut between the two beds, shutting out the horror. Lee's face was ashen. Telling him I'd be right back, I ran to the nurses' station. Obviously, someone had made a terrible mistake and assigned Lee to the wrong room. They wouldn't intentionally put a child in a room where another child was dying—and most certainly not when they had the same disease! Besides the emotional trauma, there was also the danger of infection. The doctors in the Boise and Seattle hospitals were sticklers about keeping C/F patients away from anyone they suspected of having an infection, especially another C/F patient.

At the nurses' station, I explained that an error had been made and asked that Lee be transferred to another room; I knew they had empty ones available because I'd passed two on my way to the station. The nurse looked at me as if I were crazy. There was no mistake. Whenever possible, they always roomed C/F patients together! Besides, she couldn't move Lee without permission, and the person with the authority wasn't expected back until late afternoon.

Returning to Lee, I draped his robe over his shoulders and helped him out of bed. "There's a play room down the hall," I told him. "The toys are mostly for younger kids, but it has a nice recliner and a small TV and, in case you get bored, there's a lap desk you can use to do your homework, or I can help you with some scout merit badges."

He was as anxious to get out of that room as I was, and with me pushing the I.V. stand, he shuffled down the hall and into the play area. Once he was settled in the recliner, I returned to his room to collect his belongings. Passing Robbie's bed on the way out, I whispered to his mother, "I think you and Robbie need your privacy." She nodded. Impulsively, I put my arm around her shoulders, and for a second she clung to me. Then she turned back to Robbie. I fled through the door to the play area.

I was surprised when the doctor did not immediately agree to move Lee to another room. In his opinion, my fears that Lee would get some kind of "bug" from Robbie were absolutely unfounded. He said there was no medical proof whatsoever that C/F patients transmit infections back and forth. As for my concern that it was not emotionally healthy for Lee to share a room with Robbie, I was overreacting! "Actually, C/F kids want to room together," he said. "They relate to each other."

"Do you think relating to each other is good when one of them is dying?" I cried, appalled. "If you had cancer, would you want to be in a room with a dying cancer patient?"

"Robbie isn't dying," he said irritably.

I knew I was making the doctor angry, but I pressed on. "When did you see him last?" I questioned.

For the first time, the doctor looked uncomfortable and evaded the question by answering, "Another physician is in charge of his case, but I look in on him every now and then." He stood up, dismissing me.

"What about . . ." I began.

He looked at me impatiently. "I'll look in on Robbie, and then we'll see."

Walking past Robbie's door, I glanced in. Two doctors and a bevy of nurses were crowded around him. His mother was leaning against the wall, fingers pressed tightly against her lips. Her face was white, her eyes dilated with fear.

I decided that if I had to, I would keep Lee in the play room all night and catch the first flight to the Seattle hospital in the morning rather than allow him back in that room. Happily, I didn't have to do that. Two hours later, a nurse showed us to a room where three boys were recuperating from accidents. The room was next to Robbie's, and I could hear the sound of Robbie's equipment and the murmur of doctors' voices through the thin wall.

Lee improved, and on Friday night Irene took me to her apartment at Brigham Young University in nearby Provo to stay the night. Although I was tense about leaving Lee, it was wonderful to have a break from the hospital.

When I passed Robbie's room the next morning, it was empty, the bed stripped. For Robbie, the pain and suffering were over. It was noon before Lee mentioned him. Pushing his food around on his plate, he asked, "Did Robbie die?" I nodded, and he said, "I thought so. In the night I woke up and heard his mom crying in the hall. Pretty soon a man, I guess it was his dad, came, and they went back into his room. A few minutes later his equipment stopped, and a bunch of doctors and nurses came out into the hall. One of the nurses shut our door, but I could still hear people going in and out of his room, and then there was a noise like a bed being wheeled out. I was afraid he'd died, but I was hoping they were just moving him to another floor."

I started to tell him that Robbie wasn't suffering now, that he was with his Heavenly Father. But Lee wasn't ready to talk about heaven or about Robbie. Death was still too terrifyingly real.

Lee's lung healed, and a week later Kay drove to Salt Lake and brought us home. Lee returned to school. He never mentioned Robbie.

Lee hadn't completely recovered from his collapsed lung when the pseudomonas infection struck again. This time the gentamicin shots couldn't control it, and Dr. Venning had to increase the dosage. Since the increased volume would break down too much tissue if administered by shot, it had to be adminstered intravenously. I assumed that meant hospitalization. Not so. Instead, Dr. Venning inserted a heparin lock in the vein in the back of his hand, splinted his wrist, and sent me across the street to the hospital to receive a crash course in giving I.V.'s, or "meds" as they're called by the professionals. My next stop was the drugstore. Wordlessly, I handed Dr. Venning's prescription and the list of supplies I needed to the pharmacist. Looking it over, the druggest commented, "I didn't realize you were a nurse, Mrs. Belnap." Upon hearing that I wasn't, he pursed his lips and shook his head. My already shaky confidence plummeted, and I wondered if giving meds was the "piece of cake" that the nurse had intimated it was.

It wasn't until I was home that I realized I didn't have an I.V. stand. Oh, well. I pawed through Kay's junk drawer, found a hook that looked about the right size, and pounded it into the ceiling above Lee's bed. Unable to find a rope thin enough to go through the hook and still strong enough to hold the glucose bag, I cut off the handles of an old jump rope and used that. I was gratified to see that Lee was properly impressed with my ingenuity!

With nothing else to do except wait for eleven o'clock, Lee fell asleep and my "what ifs" began. "What if" I couldn't get the drip started? The nurse said sometimes an air lock was difficult to get out of the tubing. "What if" the ride home had jiggled the catheter loose, and the medicine dripped into tissue instead of his vein? "What if" I simply called Dr. Venning and told him I wasn't cut out for this sort of thing?

Of course, the "what ifs" didn't happen. They seldom do. Still, I was relieved to have that first I.V. under my belt.

In September, Lee started South Junior High. His schoolmates in elementary school were used to him coming to school periodically with his wrist splinted, his arm in a sling. It meant he was on meds again. No big deal. However, the first time he appeared with his arm in a sling at South, his new classmates crowded around him, curious as to how he had injured it. At first he tried to explain, but, as he grumbled to me, "If I tell them the splint's to protect the heparin lock, then they want to know what a heparin lock is. That leads to why I have to have I.V.'s, and when I say it's because I have pneumonia, they ask how come I have pneumonia. That leads to having to tell them about C/F. Since none of them has ever heard of C/F, there's another avalanche of questions."

In the end, he found it simpler to say he had a sprained wrist. This explanation had its hazards, of course, because every week or ten days the doctor changed the catheter to the other wrist. He hoped his new friends wouldn't notice.

—1976—

The morning of his thirteenth birthday, Lee airily announced that since he was now a teenager, he was old enough to make his own decisions and to "start living." With that he grandly ordered pizza for dinner, gave me a peck on the cheek, and swaggered out the door.

Unfortunately, within two weeks my swaggering teenager lay in a hospital bed, looking heartbreakingly childlike. The pneumonia had struck again suddenly, beginning the morning after his birthday with a few hacking coughs. As the day wore on, the cough became deeper and more frequent, and he complained of a tightness in his chest. The next day's x-rays showed pneumonia in the lower left lobe, and we began gentamicin intravenously at home. However, instead of clearing up, the pneumonia spread into both lungs, and Dr. Venning admitted him into the hospital. Except for his hospitalization in Salt Lake with the collapsed lung, this was the first time he had been hospitalized since he was a baby. I was frightened. The treatment at the hospital was exactly the same as at home; and if it hadn't worked at home, why would it work in the hospital?

I knew Dr. Venning was worried, but he gripped Lee's shoulder and said the familiar words, "You're going to be okay, boy." Lee managed a weak grin and nod of the head. Then the doctor turned to me and ordered, "You go home and get some sleep. The nurses will take good care of him." I tried to follow his advice, but sleep eluded me, and I found myself wandering around Lee's empty room, wishing he were home so I could do battle myself. Yet, how could I "do battle" when my paltry "weapons" were seemingly no match for the disease?

Restlessly, I returned to my bed and picked up the Book of

Mormon lying on my night stand. It opened to 2 Nephi 4:34, and the words, "I will not put my trust in the arm of flesh—," leaped out at me. Had I been putting more trust in antibiotics than in the Lord? I knelt beside my bed and prayed for a long time. A week later, Dr. Venning discharged Lee to finish his meds at home.

The first thing Lee did when he walked in the door was step on the scales. Groaning loudly, he announced that he had lost seven pounds.

"That's okay, Lee," Steve consoled him. "You'll have that weight gained back and more by the time South's football practice starts this fall. Besides," he added smugly, "the coaches probably won't weigh you. They never did me. They just asked me how much I weighed, and I added an extra fifteen pounds. That's how I got to play on the heavyweight team instead of having to play lightweight."

Lee looked at his brother with admiring eyes. "Maybe if I told them I weighed an extra forty, I could play heavyweight, too," he mused optimistically. Looking at his stick-figure body, I rolled my eyes. Boys!

After two weeks on meds at home, Dr. Venning phoned and said to discontinue them. "No sense making a special trip to have me take out the heparin lock," he said off-handedly. "Just take off the splint and tape, cover the needle with gauze, and slide it out. The important thing is to keep pressure on the vein until the puncture closes and it stops bleeding."

Immediately, my imagination went into orbit, and I visualized the puncture not closing and Lee bleeding to death on the kitchen floor. Telling myself I was being ridiculous didn't help. I tried for an hour to psych myself up to the task, and then gave up. I grabbed the scissors and a package of sterile gauze and told Lee to get in the car. He was in the middle of a project and didn't want to go, especially when I wouldn't tell him where we were going. However, my stormy face convinced him to stop arguing, and he crawled into the car. When I turned into Dr. Venning's parking lot, he looked surprised. "I don't know why you couldn't have told me we were coming here. Is the doctor going to take out the needle?"

"No," I answered tersely. "I am. Give me your arm."

Puzzled, he took his arm out of the sling and scooted around in the seat until he faced me. Together, we removed the splint and inched off the tape, careful not to disturb the catheter. Now was the moment of truth. Taking a deep breath, I held the gauze firmly against the imbedded needle and slowly pulled it from his vein. Dropping the contraption into Lee's other hand, I continued to apply pressure. Much to my chagrin, only a tiny drop of blood darkened the gauze. Cutting off a fresh square, I taped it over the small red puncture, and, without a word, started the car.

We had barely driven a block when Lee, no longer able to contain himself, exploded into whoops of laughter. "You were afraid to take out the heparin lock and didn't want to tell Dr. Venning, right?" he accused, his eyes dancing with glee. "You parked in his parking lot in case you chickened out."

"I never 'chicken out' of anything," I retorted with as much dignity as I could muster.

"What then?" he asked.

"In case something went wrong, I didn't want you bleeding all over my clean house."

Lee exploded into laughter again. "Wait until I tell Dr. Venning—," he began.

"You tell a soul, and you won't be around to enjoy it," I threatened.

"Oh, sure," he chortled, enjoying my discomfort. However, he managed to control himself, and except for a wide grin and an occasional chuckle, he kept his peace. Halfway home, the absurdity of my actions hit me, and I began to smile. The smile became a grin, the grin became a chuckle, and then Lee and I were laughing crazily together. Wiping tears off my cheeks, I turned into an ice cream stand. Sliding out of the car, I said, "This isn't a bribe for your silence, you understand. It's to celebrate the meds being over."

We were companionably enjoying a root beer float when Lee observed, "Shots, I.V.'s, everything like that bothers you, doesn't it?"

I decided to be honest. "Yes," I replied. "I've been that way since I was a little girl. You'd think after all the shots and meds I've given you, I'd be completely over it, though, wouldn't you?"

"Is it a phobia?" he asked curiously.

"I wouldn't call it a phobia, exactly," I protested, not wanting to put a label on it. "Anyway, it's nothing for you to worry about. I'm okay except for an occasional lapse like today."

Sucking the last drops of root beer out of the mug, he viewed me reflectively over its rim. "You're a pretty good sport, Mom, to give me shots and I.V.'s and stuff even when you're grossed out. And I promise not to tell anyone about today." Then, eyes sparkling with merriment, he added, "But it was awfully funny."

In August, I sewed four new badges on the sash of Lee's scout uniform. They looked no more impressive than the others. All of them symbolized significant achievements in scouting. Yet, when I looked at those four, I saw more than emblems of canoeing, hiking, swimming, and lifesaving. I saw a giant leap forward in Lee's maturity.

Scouting had been an important part of Lee's life since the day three years earlier when he had watched Steve receive his Eagle Scout rank. He vowed then to do the same. The more sedentary merit badges were easy for him; the physical ones, however, were frustrating, especially the one requiring thirty consecutive days of timed physical activities. Four times he came within a day or so of completing it, only to be stopped by a lung infection. Remarkably, he didn't get discouraged, nor was he tempted to rationalize that twenty-nine days were good enough. The requirement was thirty days, and thirty days it would be.

Finally his tenacity paid off, and by the summer of 1975 he lacked only a few badges for his Eagle, badges he could easily earn at scout camp that summer. However, it was not to be, thanks to a last-minute bout with pneumonia.

This year, he was adamant that "not even the worst case of pneumonia in the world" would prevent him from going to scout camp. While admiring his determination, I was alarmed by his intensity. What a crushing blow it would be if the pseudomonas bug flared again at the last minute.

After listening to him talk about nothing but camp, camp, camp for months, we were surprised when, two weeks before camp, he stopped talking about it. In fact, he was irritable when we brought it up. Kay offered to help him get his equipment together, but he dismissed him with a curt, "I'm taking care of it." We knew something was eating at him, but we didn't know what it was until two nights before he was to leave. I was doing his treatment, and he waited until he was lying on his stomach with his face buried in his arms before he dropped the bombshell.

"Will you be disappointed in me if I don't go to scout camp?" he asked.

I was glad he couldn't see my shocked face. "Of course I wouldn't be disappointed in you, Lee," I answered quickly. "But I don't understand. Scout camp is all you've talked about for the past year. Are you getting sick?"

Irritated, he responded, "No, I'm not getting sick! Why do you always think I'm getting sick if I don't want to do something?" He changed positions on the tilt table. "You don't need to clap so hard," he grumbled. "You're pounding me to pieces. I don't see why we have to do these dumb treatments, anyway. They don't help."

With that the dam burst, and two weeks of torment poured out. "If I have to have treatments at camp, I'm not going," he said. "I'd rather stay home than have everyone gawking at me. Besides, you know that even with the new percussor, I can't do my back, and no one in the troop is going to want to take time to help me. It'll be a big mess. I don't see why I can't just skip them for a week. It wouldn't be that big a deal, and they don't do any good, anyway; I still get pneumonia."

Stories I'd heard from other parents flooded my mind—stories of youngsters sacrificing their health rather than risk being thought of as different. Until now, I hadn't worried about it. Lee was too well-adjusted, too level-headed. Or was he? After all, he was only thirteen, an age when peer approval means everything. The decision he made now could be a crucial one.

"Lee," I argued, "it isn't as if you'll be having your treatments center stage. We've made arrangements to store your equipment in the first aid room, and you can slip in there to do them. And your scoutmaster offered to do your back. None of the boys need be involved at all."

"Well, the scoutmaster changed his mind," Lee replied angrily. "Two weeks ago, right in front of all the scouts, he said that he won't have time to help with my treatments and asked for volunteers. No one offered, and I'm sure not going to beg." In a flat voice he whispered, "It was awful. I felt like puke."

While I raged silently at the scoutmaster's insensitivity, Lee continued, "I even called and asked Dr. Venning if I could skip the drainages for a week because I'd be getting lots of exercise at camp; but he said I'd accumulate too much junk in my lungs and we couldn't afford to take the risk." This revelation truly shocked me—not the doctor's stand, but that Lee had called him. Although I'd occasionally suggested it, he'd never before initiated a call to his doctor. It must have been made out of sheer desperation.

How I longed to tell him that for this one week it was okay to forget he had cystic fibrosis, that for this one week he could be a normal thirteen-year-old boy having fun at scout camp. But I couldn't do it. For thirteen years his doctors had pounded into me that daily treatments were critical. And, at his age, once the door for skipping treatments was opened, could it be closed again? I suspected not.

Lee fell silent, and I wished that I were an all-wise Solomon. Buying time, I nudged him to turn so I could clap his side. Although he faced me now, he closed his eyes, shutting me out.

He had gone as far as he was going in sharing his misery.

Taking a deep breath, I said, "Lee, Dr. Venning and Dad and I have always been straightforward with you in explaining how cystic fibrosis damages your body and why we have to fight it every day."

Eyes still closed, he interrupted rudely, "Yeah, yeah, I know all that."

"Well," I continued doggedly, "C/F can also damage your spirit, and whether it does or not depends on you. Once you begin withdrawing from things you want to do because of false pride, you open the door to letting C/F rule your life. You let it take over the Lee Belnap part of you. Is that what you want?"

Lee kept his eyes closed. I knew he was listening, but I had no idea what he was thinking. Treatment over, I gave him a hug and left the room. I hoped he would consider what I'd said.

The following morning, he announced his decision. "I've decided to go to camp," he stated. "George doesn't have much money, and maybe he'll do my back if I pay him. If the other kids see me and gawk, I guess they'll just have to gawk."

The Ore-Ida Boy Scout Camp lay sprawled on the eastern shore of the horseshoe-shaped Payette Lake in McCall, and was separated from our cabin on the western shore by a densely wooded peninsula jutting out into the middle of the lake. Wanting to be nearby in case of an emergency, but not wanting to be obvious, we arranged to take Kay's vacation at the cabin during scout camp week.

Lee wasn't due in camp until Monday, but Friday after work Kay, Steve, Roger, Lee, and I drove to the cabin. On the drive up, we made elaborate plans for the coming week—plans which were changed on Sunday night by a knock on the cabin door. It was the McCall Fish and Game warden. Kay was needed in Boise early the next morning and would have to leave that night. Since their dad would be returning to McCall on Wednesday, Roger and Steve decided to go back with him and play in a baseball tournament scheduled for Tuesday evening.

In the hurried confusion of getting Kay and the two boys off, no one remembered that I was being left without a car, and that my only means to transport Lee and his belongings across the lake was the boat.

Lee had driven the boat for years, and getting to the camp was no problem. The problem was getting me back. With seven children clamoring to drive, I'd never felt the need to learn. But obviously there was a need now, and it couldn't have come at a worse time. Outside, dusk was setting in, and an unseasonably cold rain was beginning to drizzle. However, the teaching lesson couldn't wait, so we bundled ourselves into our rain gear and made our way down the slippery path to the dock. There, Lee gave me a crash course in driving and docking a boat.

Starting the motor and steering was a snap, but docking the boat, a maneuver which looked deceptively simple when executed by Kay and the children, was quite another matter. I quickly discovered that docking a boat at a dock that bucked to and fro at the whim of every passing wave was not in the least like parking a car at a concrete curb. Lee patiently showed me the maneuver over and over again.

"The trick," he said pointing to the shoreline, "is to aim the bow at that tree, and when you get to within about twenty feet of it, pull back the throttle and twist the wheel to the left until the boat is at right angles to the dock. Let the bow get within a few feet of the dock, and then turn hard to the left again until the boat and dock are parallel. Shift into neutral, and the waves will rock the boat the final inches to the dock. As soon as you nudge the dock, turn off the motor, leap out before it drifts away, and secure the boat. That's all there is to it." It sounded easy, and probably for everyone else in the world it was. But not for me. In the first place, through the drizzling rain, one tree looked like every other tree, and judging distances was never my forte.

Doggedly, I kept practicing. First I would come in too slow and too far away from the dock, and the next time I would come in too fast and too close, causing Lee to scream and grab the wheel, barely saving his dad from returning to a bottomless boat. I gradually improved, but I still needed more practice. The problem was that even with our boat lights on, it was becoming dangerously dark on the lake. We decided to get up early the next morning and continue the tutorage. Wet and cold, we trudged back up the dark, winding path, slipping in the mud and stumbling over half-buried roots.

The cabin had never seemed more inviting. Lee threw another log on the fire; and after changing into dry, warm clothes, we sat toasting our feet and sipping hot chocolate laced with miniature marshmallows. I was too tired to worry about Lee catching cold from our night's adventure or about whether or not, when the time came, I could dock the boat on my own. It was enough that I was warm and dry and didn't have to face anything for several more hours.

Morning came all too soon; and, although it was chilly with an overcast sky, at least the rain had stopped during the night, and I gave thanks for that. Drainage completed, Lee disinfected and packed his equipment while I cooked him a substantial breakfast of bacon, eggs, and pancakes. I settled for orange juice and a slice of toast. The thought of what lay ahead made my stomach queazy.

Together we toted the portable tilt table, the compressor, nebulizer, and assorted aerosols and medications down the path and stashed them in the boat. By the time we added a sleeping bag, clothes, and scouting gear, there was scarcely room for us.

Unlike the night before, the lake was calm except for occasional waves created by passing boats. My first two docking practices were marginal, but my third try was rewarded with a big grin and thumbs-up from my coach. It was time for the real thing.

To give me additional hands-on experience, I drove the boat until we neared the camp, and then Lee took over. It wouldn't do for a scout to be seen being delivered by his mother—especially one who might land us on top of the dock!

We were carrying the last load of equipment into camp when Lee's troop arrived from Boise. When they discovered that I was returning to the cabin by boat, ALL BY MYSELF, they eyed me with new respect and escorted me to the dock to see me off. Feigning a confidence I didn't feel, I slid behind the wheel, turned on the motor, slipped the boat into gear, and would have departed with the dock except for Lee's warning cry. While he untied me, I prayed that the story of how Mom almost made off with the dock in front of the whole scout troop wouldn't become a popular campfire tale for years to come. I suspected that it would.

On Wednesday, Kay and the boys came back from Boise, and that evening we made a quick run over to see how Lee was faring. His dad and brothers climbed the hill to the camp while I stayed in the boat, sparing him the humiliation of being checked on by his mother. (Dads and brothers were always welcome, mothers and sisters never.) They found Lee in the first aid room, where his treatment was being handled with military precision. A small scout with an uncombed mop of red hair and a face full of freckles acted as timekeeper, shouting, "turn" the second a lobe received its allotted time, while a more hefty scout, his body bursting the seams of a uniform which had undoubtedly fit him perfectly the year before, enthusiastically manned the percussor at top speed. Meanwhile, a third scout disinfected Lee's mask and nebulizer. Still another quarterbacked from the doorway, counting down the minutes before they were due to play for the volleyball championship. If this was any indication, drainages were definitely not the social problem Lee had feared. Dirty and happy, with no time to talk to family, he was one happy scouter.

September was a month of more family changes, with Steve leaving for college at the beginning of the month and Stan returning from his mission and later joining Steve at BYU.

When it was time for us to leave Steve at his residence hall, he walked us to our car. He embraced his father, gave me a big hug and kiss, and turned to Lee. To hide their emotions, they traded insults, playfully punched each other on the arm a few times, and then it was time to go.

Steve stood at the curb watching us pull away, and Lee and I waved to him until we turned a corner. No longer able to see his brother, Lee straightened around in his seat and announced that he was going to take a nap. A few minutes later I glanced back. His eyes were closed, but tears were running silently down his cheeks. Home wouldn't be the same for him without his Steve.

Lee stuffed himself all summer, hoping he would weigh enough for heavyweight football at South Junior High in the fall. To his dismay, when the weighing-in day came, he weighed only sixty-six pounds—four pounds less than before his bout with pneumonia in the spring. He settled for lightweights, and even then the coach was hard-pressed to find a uniform small enough to fit him. Boys his size usually didn't choose to play football! However, after I took in the waist and hemmed up the pant legs, the bottoms fit fairly well. The top, with its bulky shoulder pads, drowned him. Nevertheless, he was happy. He was a member of a football team, and it didn't matter that week after week he mostly sat out the games on the bench. He lived for those few minutes he was allowed to play.

Then came the final game of the season. It was against South's arch rival and the only other undefeated junior high school team in the city. It was bound to be a close game, and in close games the coach rarely substituted players. However, neither that nor the fact that Dr. Venning hadn't let him practice for a week because of a lung infection kept Lee from dreaming that the coach would put him in, and that he'd make a game-winning play. Every day after school, he faithfully suited up to sit alone on the bench, watching his teammates scrimmage, clinging to the hope that by game time the doctor would give him permission to play.

All the way to Dr. Venning's office on the morning of the big game, he assured me between bouts of coughing that he felt much better and was sure that he was well enough to play.

With shining eyes, he confided, "Before I got sick, Coach said he had a trick play up his sleeve and had me practice catching long bombs. I must say I did pretty good, too, thanks to all the practice I had with Steve this summer."

It was a silent and despondent Lee who sat beside me as I drove him back to school. His lungs were still full of infection, and the doctor had told him he couldn't play. Getting out of the car, he mumbled morosely, "Don't bother to come to the game. Since I can't play, I may as well not even suit up." Before I could reply, he shut the car door. Watching him walk through the school door, his head down, my heart ached for him. Why did he have to love sports so much?

That afternoon, waiting for him to come home, I tried to think of some consoling remarks. I needn't have bothered. He came through the door positively "hyper"! His eyes glowed, and his cheeks were so flushed that I automatically felt his forehead for a fever. He shook off my hand, stumbling over his words as he told me about South's exciting come-from-behind victory in the final minutes of the game. "You should have seen our quarterback throw the pass that set up the touchdown. Their defense was caught flat-footed," he gloated. "*Nobody* expected it."

I was so relieved that he was in high spirits that it didn't occur to me to ask who caught the pass or why "nobody expected it." That evening a friend who had attended the game called, and I found out. Of course, *no one* would expect a coach to send in the smallest kid on his team on a fourth down in the final minutes of a game and then instruct the quarterback to throw him a long bomb! However, that's just what he did; and the quarterback, in his longest and most accurate pass of the season, threw the ball to Lee, who was all alone at the fifteen-yard line. Lee jumped high in the air, hauled it in, and managed to run ten yards before being smothered by the defense—not a touchdown, but close enough to set one up for the next play.

When I asked Lee why he hadn't told us he was the one who made the catch, he answered sheepishly, "I was working up to it.

I guess I was a little worried that you might let it slip to Dr. Venning, and he'd be mad at me." To his credit, Lee hadn't intended to disregard his doctor's orders. He had, in fact, dutifully informed his coach that he couldn't play and that he wasn't going to suit up. His coach, busy checking his roster, grunted and said that was too bad; but, since it was the last game, he should suit up anyway and sit on the bench with the team.

During the post-game revelry, the coach slapped Lee and the quarterback on their seats and congratulated them on a good play, just like it was an every-game occurrence. However, I suspect he was as stunned as the opposing coach when Lee actually came down with the football. I don't know why he sent Lee in, but I like to think that he felt one quick play wouldn't hurt him; and, if by a miracle he made the catch, he'd feel rewarded for all those weeks he'd sat on the bench. And he was right. Lee remembered that play the rest of his life.

Lee became an Eagle Scout at age 14,
and also played football at South Junior High.

—1977—

In February we left Steve at the Language Training Center in Provo, Utah, to study Portuguese for a few weeks before leaving for his mission to Sao Paulo, Brazil. His body was tense when I kissed him goodbye, and my heart went out to this reserved son of mine. New situations had always been difficult for him; yet, when the mission call came to go to Brazil, he didn't hesitate.

Steve and Lee tried to act "cool," but when they gave each other one last punch on the arm, tears filled Steve's eyes and Lee's chin quivered. Steve had helped Lee over many a hurdle, and they were best buddies as well as brothers. Two years looked like a long time.

On our way home, we stopped at the University of Utah C/F Clinic to have Lee checked. Although I knew he needed periodic checkups at the clinic, I dreaded those visits, fearing that he would pick up a new "bug" from another C/F patient.

In the C/F treatment room, out-patients as well as many of the hospitalized C/F patients received their treatments. The room was small and looked as if it may have been a small storage room or walk-in closet at one time. This day, as usual, it bulged with C/F patients suffering varying degrees of lung involvement. Three little girls, about five years of age, sat around a small table, playing Yahtze and coughing in each other's faces. At the back of the room, an older boy was using a nebulizer while a sandy-haired lad beside him used the IPP machine. Periodically, they spit thick, greenish-brown mucus into disposable paper cups.

A young teenaged boy, connected to an oxygen tank, sat hunched forward in a chair in a corner, his head buried in a book, waiting for his turn on the tilt table. Every few minutes his reading was interrupted by violent, unproductive coughing that left him breathless. On this floor, violent coughing was so common that no one even glanced at him, and as soon as he caught his breath he returned to his book.

On the other side of the room, a young, long-legged inhalation therapist in a white coat, stethoscope dangling from her neck, bent over a little girl lying head down on the tilt table. Clad in light blue jeans and a plaid shirt, dark hair pulled back in a pony tail, the youngster strained to cough. The therapist clapped her harder and she coughed up a glob of dark, blood-streaked mucus. A little boy nearby shouted, "That's showing Mr. Gunk who's boss!"

On our way down the hall from the treatment room, we passed a mother pushing a small boy in a wheelchair, an oxygen mask strapped to his face. Her eyes were bright with unshed tears, but she managed to pull her lips into an artificial smile as she passed us. Her little passenger was cyanotic, and his wasted body sagged weakly against the restraining straps of the wheelchair. Lee and I walked faster and faster until we were almost running toward the exit that led to the cold, outside winter air and away from the sights and sounds of impending death.

In May, Kay had heart bypass surgery. During the week he was recuperating in one wing of the hospital, Jim McGinnis and Rick Cochran died in another. Lee scarcely knew Jim, but he knew Rick Cochran well. Rick was a member of the Red Rock Christian Church, but in his healthier days he had enjoyed playing basketball with our church team. Lee attended the games and watched this older C/F boy with great interest. Here was a C/F boy doing it all. He was actively engaged in a fast-paced sport, getting top grades in school, and was well liked by his peer group. If Rick could do it, he could do it, too.

There was no good way to tell a fourteen-year-old that two of his C/F comrades had passed away, especially when he had tried to emulate one of them. When I tried to put my arms around him, he stepped back, saying, "I'm going to ride my bike. I'll be back in a while." Alarmed when he wasn't home for dinner, I sent

Roger looking for him. He couldn't find him; and, after we'd eaten, I sent him on to the hospital to visit his father while I waited for Lee. When Lee returned, his eyes were red and swollen. I hoped he would share his pain, but he only said, "I'm not hungry. I'll be in my room."

At Rick's funeral, Reverend Thornton told the congregation the same remarkable story about Rick's death that Rick's mother had shared with me earlier. Rick had died, and then came back to life again without medical intervention. He told his parents he had gone through a long tunnel, and when he reached the end, relatives welcomed him. Upon finding himself back in his hospital room, he was confused and frightened until, as he related to his parents, he was told not to be afraid. They weren't ready for him, but they would come again when it was time. A few minutes later he slipped peacefully away. This time he did not return. Looking at his parents' serene faces at the cemetery, I thought how blessed they were to have had this beautiful spiritual experience.

In order to keep pace with our rising medical expenses, in July I began working five hours a day as a secretary for Ron Thurber, an architect and long-time friend. It was the perfect job for me. Ron understood Lee's medical needs and allowed me to juggle my hours around them when I needed to.

In August, Lee received his Eagle Scout Recognition Award. My eyes were not the only moist ones in the room when his father, an Eagle Scout himself, slipped the Eagle neckerchief around his neck and saluted him.

As I watched, I reflected on the years Lee had blessed our lives. It seemed a lifetime ago, and yet, paradoxically, only yesterday, that I had sat in Dr. Venning's office following Lee's first hospitalization. At that time, the doctor wondered aloud if it would not have been better for all, including Lee, if he had succumbed to that first bout of pneumonia. How terribly ill he'd been, and how utterly hopeless it seemed in those early days when one doctor after another predicted that he would not live to reach his second birthday. Yet, here he was, fourteen years old and the happy recipient of the Eagle Badge, a recognition given to him not because the committee felt sorry for him, but because he was a determined, hard-working scout who had fulfilled each and every requirement.

Except for a few minor skirmishes with lung infections, Lee had an "unremarkable" year with his health until the night before Christmas, when he had a violent coughing spell. I hurried to his room and found him sitting on the edge of his bed, feet dangling over the side. His temperature was 104 degrees. However, that didn't alarm me nearly as much as his shortness of breath. Every three hours I gave him an inhalation and postural drainage treatment with no measurable success. At one point, he said fervently, "I sure hope Dr. Venning isn't out of town for Christmas." I agreed.

Unfortunately, he was. However, his associate agreed to see us, and early Christmas morning, we drove through a light snowstorm to his office. He listened to Lee's lungs and talked briefly about hospitalizing him. In the end, he wrote out a prescription for an antibiotic and told me to call Dr. Venning on Tuesday. We were almost out the door before I remembered the pharmacies would be closed. "Just call any pharmacy," he said, "and your call will be transferred to an emergency number."

Wrong! It was not until I was nearly through the "O's" in the yellow pages that I connected with a human being. The woman who answered sounded young and excited, and in the background I could hear loud squeals of laughter and the sound of ripping paper. I knew I had interrupted a young family in the midst of opening Christmas gifts. The woman said she'd meet me at the pharmacy in forty-five minutes.

The snow was falling hard by now, but traffic was light and I made good time. Arriving first, I swung into the deserted parking lot and parked in front of the pharmacy. It was located in the middle of a normally busy shopping center, but today the buildings were dark and empty. I turned off the motor and killed my car lights. Looking about uneasily, I reached over and locked the car doors. In a few minutes, two bright lights turned into the parking lot, and a pickup parked a few spaces down from me. A woman, restraining a doberman pinscher, stepped out of the truck and studied my car. I rolled down the window and called out, "Are you the pharmacist? I'm the woman who phoned."

"I am," she acknowledged. "Give me a minute, and I'll let you in." She and the dog disappeared inside. In a few minutes, the store was ablaze with light and she was at the door, motioning to me. Once I was inside, she quickly locked the door behind me. I noted that the dog remained close by her side. I apologized for taking her away from her family on Christmas, and she gave me a quick nod and said that she hoped I didn't mind the dog. When it was her turn to open for an emergency, she took him along.

Minutes after I arrived home, the phone rang. It was Dr. Venning. He had checked in with his associate and discovered that Lee was ill. He doubted if the antibiotic would work, but as long as Lee was on it, he guessed it would do until he could run some cultures on Tuesday. In the meantime, if Lee became worse, I was to call him in Twin Falls, and he would return immediately. I hung up the phone, greatly relieved that he was only two hours away. Over the years, Dr. Venning had pulled Lee through many a crisis; and along the way, he had become a personal friend as well as Lee's physician. I couldn't believe that once I had thought him gruff.

—1978—

Lee objected strenuously when Dr. Venning hospitalized him the day after New Year's. "Why the hospital?" he demanded. "I'm not that sick, and I have school."

"We've no choice," Dr. Venning answered shortly. "Your white count is 21,800 and your sed rate is 57. The pneumonia is infiltrating your front lobes as well as the back. I want you in the hospital." Lee and I trudged gloomily across the street to St. Luke's. It had been nearly two years since his last hospitalization, and I wondered what he was thinking. During the interim, had he started believing that he had C/F licked, or at least under control?

Lee was nervous about missing school, especially with finals coming up; and every day I went to South Junior High to pick up and return assignments. All except two of his teachers cooperated beautifully. However, those two had the attitude that if he wasn't in class when they reviewed the material, too bad. They refused to give me even skeleton outlines of material they were covering. I wondered if their attitude would soften if they were to see him in the hospital, lips blue, an I.V. needle in his arm, doggedly doing homework in spite of the pounding pneumonia-induced headache and the cough that nearly turned his body inside out. Looking at his dull, sunken eyes, I tried to get him to stop worrying about school and devote his energies toward getting well, but he was too much of a student to do that.

Then, overnight, his attitude changed. He swung from being overly concerned about school to showing no interest at all. Instead of looking forward to visits from his friends, he asked them not to come. He quit eating. Not even his favorite dishes from home tempted him. He pushed them aside, saying, "I'm not hungry; I'll eat later."

Dr. Venning also noted the change and called me at the office. "I think we'd better get Lee out of the hospital," he said. "He's depressed, and that isn't at all like him. Maybe he's homesick, I don't know. At any rate, all the fight has gone out of him, and that's not good. His lungs aren't as clear as I'd like and his sed rate is still high; but I think he'll do better at home now. I've called in a prescription for tetracycline."

Minutes later, Lee called. "Dr. Venning is stopping my meds and said I can go home. Can you leave work right now and come get me?" When I arrived, he was sitting tensely on the edge of his bed, his packed bag beside him. He kept his eyes glued on the door while we waited for the nurse's aid to bring the wheelchair. Every few minutes he demanded, "What's taking her so long?" During the drive home, I tried to make small talk, but he sat as rigid as a board, staring straight ahead, answering only in mono-syllables. Once in his room, he wandered around opening and closing closet drawers and fingering the knick-knacks on his dresser. He was still tense that evening during his drainage, his muscles tight beneath my fingers. Afterward, I sat on the edge of his bed and rubbed his back, trying to help him relax. Finally, he fell into a troubled sleep.

At midnight I took him his medicine. He started violently when I touched his shoulder, protecting his left forearm where the I.V. had been. "It's okay," I whispered. "The I.V.'s out. You're home, and I've brought you your medicine." I helped him sit up and handed him the capsule and a glass of water. "Everything's okay," I repeated. "Take your pill and go back to sleep."

He swallowed the pill obediently, and I took his glass. Then he looked around the room as if he couldn't believe he was actually there. "I'm really home, aren't I?" he whispered. "I didn't die in the hospital, after all."

Surprise shot through me like an electric shock. "Lee, what do you mean, you didn't die after all?"

He looked startled, as if unaware that he had spoken aloud.

"Oh, nothing," he muttered. "Just something someone said."

I pressed him for more information. "Who said what, and when?"

Uncomfortable, he mumbled, "I overheard my nurse tell someone in the hall that I wasn't going to make it out of the hospital."

Shaken, I continued my inquisition. "Tell me exactly what you heard. Did she call you by name?"

"Well, no, she didn't say my name, but she was right outside my door so she had to be talking about me. I don't remember her words exactly, but it was something like, 'I've never cared for a terminal patient this young before. I just hope he doesn't die on my shift.'"

"Lee," I gasped, "she may have been outside your door, but she wasn't talking about you. You had a stubborn case of pneumonia, but you were far from terminal." Sickened by what he must have gone through, I cried, "I can't believe you didn't tell me this before. Why didn't you say something at the hospital?"

He looked down. "I guess I thought you knew and didn't want me to know." Then, raising his eyes, he looked me squarely in the face. "I want you to promise me something, Mom. When I'm dying, I want you and Dad to tell me flat out, no lying or pretending that I'm okay. You can't imagine how awful it is to think you're dying and not be able to talk about it to anyone because you aren't supposed to know. I've never been so lonesome in my whole life."

My throat constricted, but I managed to keep my voice steady. "I promise. But I want you to promise me something, too. Promise that when you're troubled, no matter what the reason, you'll come to either your father or me. It may be totally unrelated to C/F; it may be something we may not fully understand, even something that will cause us great pain; but promise to come to us."

He promised. Then, embarrassed at having revealed such personal feelings, he said, "You can go back to bed now and get some sleep. I'm okay."

Back in my bed, I reflected on the promise I had made. When the time came, would I have the strength to keep it? And should I? What if telling him extinguished his last spark of fight, the fight that might keep him alive? Did I or anyone else have the right to do that? Yet, what about his rights? Didn't he have the right to share the loneliness of dying with those he loved?

Unable to sleep, I tiptoed into his room. He was sleeping soundly. I leaned over and tucked the blanket more snugly around his shoulders. He looked so very young lying there—far too young to be concerned about death. My arms ached to cradle him as I had when he was a small child; but instead, I brushed his cheek with my lips and inwardly prayed, "Please, let the cure be discovered in time."

Dr. Venning allowed Lee to return to school at the end of January, but the infection continued to simmer in his lungs. His gaunt face and the deep black circles under his eyes bore silent witness to the toll it was taking on his body. Still, through the long winter he continued to attend early morning church seminary and participate in school and church activities. Finally spring arrived, and with it the good news that the infection was under control and we could discontinue the antibiotics and twice-weekly blood tests. We heaved a collective sigh of relief.

Nearly fifteen, Lee was not as open now about C/F as he had once been, and I was surprised when he accepted an insurance underwriter's invitation to speak about it at a luncheon. He did an excellent job. After briefly explaining what C/F was and its effect on the body, he showed slides Steve had made years before when he had given a presentation on C/F in a health class. To illustrate the treatments involved, Lee showed a slide of himself studying at his desk, his face hidden behind a nebulizing mask. He compared draining glue-like mucus out of his lungs to getting thick catsup out of a small-necked bottle, and he included a slide of himself head down on the tilt table getting his chest pounded. When he came to fighting lung infections with antibiotics, there was a comic slide of me chasing him with a needle, followed by one of him lying in a hospital bed, an I.V. in his arm.

Pausing after the hospital shot, he said, "C/F may be something that I live with, but it's not my life. Now I want to show you the *real* me."

The first slide was of a macho Lee sitting behind the wheel of his dad's pickup. Another showed him dressed in his South Junior High band uniform, trumpet in hand, smiling broadly into the camera. Of course, there had to be one of him riding his bike to baseball practice, glove prominently displayed on the handlebars, as well as one in his football uniform, squinting into the sun, helmet dangling from his fingers. In another he was in a dirty, rumpled scout uniform cooking bacon and eggs over an open fire; and in the final one he was in his suit posing with the bishop outside the church. His point: he was a normal teenager who happened to have cystic fibrosis.

At the end of the presentation, he asked if anyone had questions. There were many, and I was amazed at the ease and professionalism with which he handled them. He would have done a C/F specialist proud! He summed up his presentation by saying, "While I've never tried to hide the fact I have C/F, I don't dwell on it and don't like others to, either. Fighting C/F is a necessary part of my life. I accept that, and as I get older I take more and more responsibility for my own care, preparing for the time when I leave home for college." When he sat down, the one hundred fifty field underwriters rose as one in a standing ovation, many with tears in their eyes as they saluted him.

In July, Stan married lovely Sylvia Hanks in the Idaho Falls Temple. How handsome he looked as he knelt across from his beautiful bride! Driving back to our hotel after the reception, Lee said, "Just think, in a few years I'll be marrying a cute little chick like Sylvia."

A month later we drove Roger down to Ricks College in southeastern Idaho, and there was another empty bedroom at home.

Lee tried to pretend that his first day of high school was no big deal, but when you're getting your chest clapped, it's hard to disguise a racing heart and tense muscles!

He must have changed his shirt at least a half dozen times before he doused himself liberally with Brut, practiced his "cool" look in the mirror one more time, and banged out the door, remembering in mid-stride that it wasn't cool to appear eager when you're in high school. Halting his headlong rush, he sauntered to the car, scowled, flicked an imaginary speck of dust off the door (in case the girl next door was watching), and slid into the driver's seat. Acknowledging my wave with a kingly nod in my direction, he slipped the car into gear and drove away to pick up two of his friends, having won the toss for the honor of being the carpool driver on the first day of high school. My youngest child in high school. Unbelievable!

In spite of his bypass heart surgery, Kay's heart condition worsened steadily, and in mid-September, his cardiologist told him that he must quit his job. We accepted Mary's offer to give Lee his treatments, and Kay and I retreated to the cabin in McCall for the weekend. We needed to be alone in a peaceful place to collect ourselves and make some hard decisions, and McCall was peaceful this time of year. The summer people had boarded up their cabins and returned to their homes for the winter; and, except for the occasional whine of a chain saw as a winter resident added to his woodpile and the honking of geese circling the lake on their flight south, all was quiet.

We sat in front of the fireplace all afternoon and late into the night, pencils in hand, working with hard facts and figures, exploring and discarding one option after another. Among the options we discussed and dismissed was selling the cabin. Real estate prices in McCall were depressed at the time, and selling it would only be a short-term fix. We needed a long-term solution. In the end, we reluctantly acknowledged that which we'd known from the beginning. I would have to work full-time at a higher paying job. Financially, we had no choice.

Depressed, Kay went to bed while I continued to sit in front of the fireplace, watching the fire burn itself out. The cabin rapidly became cold, but still I stared into the dying embers. How was I going to care for Lee and work full-time?

But we do what we have to do, and for the next ten and a half years I worked full-time for Grant Ipsen at Mutual of New York.

In mid-December, my phone rang itself off the hook with jubilant friends calling to see if I'd read that a cure for C/F had been found! Their excitement was caused by a UPI article in the newspaper in which a St. Louis veterinary pathologist, Dr. Joel D. Wallach, was quoted as saying, "C/F, a deadly disease of children long thought to be a genetic disorder, actually is caused by a nutritional deficiency during pregnancy and can be cured." The article was lengthy, but the gist of it was that cystic fibrosis could be prevented by proper diet and could be cured by surgery in some cases and with selenium in others.

Neither Lee nor I had seen the article before he hurried off to school, and it didn't occur to me that he would hear about it before I had the chance to discuss it with him. But he did. He burst through the door, his voice shrill with excitement. "Did you hear the news, Mom? They have a cure for C/F!" Before I could answer, he danced me around the kitchen, shouting, "No more C/F, no more coughing my insides out, no more treatments, no more wondering when it's going to get me."

I hope there's a special place in hell reserved for those who sensationalize unsubstantiated cures for terminal diseases. However, even if there is, it can never be as bitter as the hell I went through watching the light go out of my young son's eyes when I explained that, while it "might" be true, as yet the "cure" was an unlikely theory.

Three days after Christmas, Kay, Lee, and I said goodbye to Roger as he entered the Language Training Center in Provo to begin a two-year mission to the Spanish-speaking people in Anaheim, California. Only yesterday he had been a cuddly little brown-eyed toddler crawling into my lap for loves! Now he was a broad-shouldered young man, going into the world to preach the gospel. On the way home, Lee tried to make a joke about being an only child now, but his voice cracked and he gave up. He would miss his brother sorely, as we all would.

Lee loved to wear his "Sherlock Holmes" hat.

—1979—

Although Lee couldn't compete on a high school level, he continued his love affair with sports by participating in church softball and basketball.

Only seven boys, including Lee, went out for the junior basketball team the winter of 1979, but they played well, and at the end of the season they had earned a berth in the regional tournament. Lee was walking on air. This would be his first time to play at region. Unfortunately, he came down with a lung infection shortly before the tournament started, and the first night of competition found him in the cheering section rather than on the floor. He fully expected to be there the second night also; but by game time only five players were in the gym, including Lee and Drew Frogley, who had a badly sprained ankle.

Expecting the other two players any second, the coach asked the two boys to suit up in order to avoid a forfeit. They quickly changed; and at the sound of the buzzer, the required five players were on the floor. Lee avoided looking at me. He knew that playing basketball with pneumonia was definitely a "no-no," and I would be less than happy with him. He was right about that. However, since I couldn't bodily remove him from the floor, I consoled myself with the thought that all they needed was a warm body for a few minutes until the other boys came, and he would take it easy until then. But the other boys didn't come, and Lee was too much of a competitor to take it easy. I don't know how he did it, but he was all over the floor, sticking like glue to the boy he was guarding, jumping high in the air to steal passes, racing down the floor and passing the ball off like an efficient little machine. Soon, I was on my feet screaming with the rest of the ward.

Unbelievably, the game was neck-and-neck until the last quarter. By then, Drew was reduced to hopping on one foot, and Lee was completely drained. The three healthy players tried to pick up the slack, but the other team spurted ahead and won handily. At the final buzzer, Drew and Lee leaned against each other and collapsed in a heap on the floor. They had, somehow, hung on for the entire game. To celebrate a moral, if not an actual victory, we took the boys to a pizza parlor where they rehashed the game and wolfed down pizza and root beer. Watching Lee reach for his third slice, I thought, "Not only has he played basketball with pneumonia, but he's also eating pizza without enzymes. We're asking for big trouble." Then I looked at his glowing face and knew that for him, it was worth it.

Lee enjoyed a comparatively good winter and spring, but in May he was hospitalized again with pneumonia. Most of his hospitalizations lasted at least two weeks, and I was surprised when at the end of the first week I walked into his room and found him sitting on the edge of his bed, a big grin on his face. "Dr. Venning says I can go home this afternoon," he announced, shoving a paper into my hand. "I'll be on meds for another two weeks, so we'll need these. Dr. Venning will call and tell you when to come after me."

Shortly after noon, Dr. Venning called, but not to release him. Instead, he said, "We have a calamity going on over here. Lee's kidneys have quit functioning, probably a side effect of the gentamicin. I've called a kidney specialist, and he should be here any minute." I thought I would never reach the hospital. I must have hit every red light, and each one seemed an hour long.

At the hospital, Dr. Venning was furious. He said that it wasn't until the nurse had asked Lee for a urine specimen and he couldn't give her one that they realized he hadn't "gone" since the afternoon before. "If they'd been measuring his output like they're supposed to when he's on gentamicin, we'd have known something was wrong and wouldn't have given him the last two I.V.'s," he raged. "This is terrible, just terrible." He looked at his watch.

"That kidney fellow should be here any minute, and then we'll know just how bad this is." He walked out the door, shaking his head and repeating, "This is terrible, just terrible." Seconds later he was back in Lee's room gripping his shoulder. "But don't you worry, boy," he said. "You're going to be okay."

Lee attempted a feeble joke. "That's a relief," he replied. "For a minute there, I thought there would be weeping and wailing among the girls at Borah High!"

The kidney specialist came, and there was talk about dialysis; but in the end they decided to wait.

When we were alone Lee grumbled, "I don't see what the big deal is. So I don't have to 'go' right now. Except for a head and back ache, I'm not hurting anyplace. When I have to go, I'll go." True to his word, later that evening he "went," but there was no more talk of an early release. Saying that he must never again be given gentamicin, Dr. Venning prescribed carbenicillin to be administered intravenously every six hours.

Lee was still in the hospital on Memorial Day weekend, and Saturday evening he started fidgeting and glancing at his watch. About 8:00 o'clock he suggested that since I was probably tired, I could go home and rest.

"I'm okay," I answered, surprised at his sudden concern. "With Dad and Steve at the cabin, there's no reason for me to hurry home. We may as well watch TV and keep each other company."

When my suggestion met with a noticeable lack of enthusiasm, I decided to give him his space. Waiting for the elevator, I caught a glimpse of two of his friends peeking around the corner of the corridor. When they saw me, they quickly stepped back out of sight. Was it my imagination, or did I smell pizza? I was tempted to linger and see what they were up to, but then decided I really didn't want to know. Whatever it was, Lee was in on it.

When I opened the door to Lee's room the next morning, the reek of stale pizza nearly knocked me off my feet. Lee's words tumbled over each other as he crowed about how his friend,

David Callister, and three girls from Borah had "snuckered" the nurses. "They put the pizza in an empty game box and smuggled it into my room," he chortled gleefully. "The nurses didn't have a clue. One even passed them in the hall, but she just glanced at the game box and reminded them visiting hours were over."

Remembering the smell of pizza wafting down the hall as I'd waited for the elevator, I doubted that the nurses "didn't have a clue."

He laughed again, reliving the joke. "They stayed until the inhalation therapist came at nine o'clock to give me my treatment. He was a neat guy. He said if we'd give him a piece, he wouldn't tell. By the way," he added, opening his drawer and pulling out a slice of cold, greasy pizza wrapped in an equally greasy napkin, "Happy Birthday! I couldn't get out to buy you a present, but I saved you this."

That summer, Lee worked as a "go-fer" for Paul Proctor, a general construction contractor. Due at work by 6:00 a.m. each morning, he set his alarm for 4:30 in order to complete his treatment and have breakfast. Kay and I worried about him overdoing, but he was so pleased to have a job and be making his own spending money that we decided to wait and see how he held out.

One morning, Mr. Proctor flew him in his small plane to McCall to help Kay rewire the cabin. Lee came home with his head filled with dreams. He was going to be a pilot—if not for a commercial airline, then for Morrison-Knudsen, or Boise Cascade, or even the Fish & Game Department. If he was ever aware of anything self-defeating about planning to become a pilot while I was pounding his back to help him breathe, he gave no indication.

High School Band and Drill Team Competition among the participants in Idaho is Super Bowl Sunday, the NBA Championship games, and the Olympics all rolled into one. Early morning and evening practices begin before school starts in the fall and continue on an escalating scale until the big night.

During the week preceding Competition, the students whip themselves into a competitive frenzy with activities ranging all the way from pep assemblies to bonfire rallies.

Next in importance to Competition itself was the dress rehearsal for parents and friends; and Kay and I, dressed in parkas, gloves, and lined boots to ward off the cold, joined hundreds of other Borah parents on the practice field. There we yelled and clapped our appreciation for the music and the precisely-executed routines that bore testimony to the hundreds of arduous hours of practice.

"I hope it isn't this cold tomorrow night when you perform, or you'll freeze to death," I worried to Lee as we hurried to the car after the performance.

"At least it isn't raining," he answered, blowing on half-frozen fingers. I didn't even want to think about that. He was already stretching his luck to participate in the cold. In a freezing rain, it would be out of the question. Looking up at a sky filled with stars, I was relieved that there wasn't a cloud in the sky.

But during the night, clouds moved in; and when my alarm went off at 5:00 a.m., rain was drumming on the patio roof and bouncing off the paved road in front of our house. I hurried to wake Lee and found him in the family room, his nebulizer already going. "It's raining," I said by way of greeting.

"Yeah, I know," he answered, his voice muffled by the mask covering his nose and mouth. "It started about an hour ago. I hope it stops soon or the turf will be really slick. It would be definitely uncool to slip and land on my duff in front of a stadium full of people. Definitely uncool, that."

"Definitely," I agreed, eying him grimly. "But not nearly as uncool as if you march in a freezing rain and end up in the hospital. That would not only be uncool, but downright dumb."

He looked at me, disbelief darkening his face as my words sank in. "Mom! You're not hinting that if it's raining tonight, I shouldn't march, are you?" His voice rose. "This is *Competition*. I can't drop out at the last minute. I'd be letting everybody down!

It's not that I'm that good, but if I'm not there, there'll be a hole on the field, and the judges will take points off. We'd lose, and all because I was afraid of a little rain."

"Don't be silly," I said more briskly than I felt. "We're talking about more than a little rain. We're talking about a freezing rain that could put you in the hospital with pneumonia for who knows how long. Anyway, I doubt if judges take points off when someone is unavoidably absent."

Lee, looking wretched, finished the nebulization in silence and then hoisted himself onto the tilt table, where he laid head down on his stomach while I clapped his back. We were nearly through when he sat up and swung his legs over the side of the tilt table. "Mom," he said, "I don't think you understand that this is about more than marching in the rain. Do you remember when I was thirteen and told you I wasn't going to scout camp because I was afraid the other scouts would poke fun at me when I had my treatments? You said then that C/F might cripple my body; but, unless I let it, it could never cripple my spirit. Well, that night I vowed that I was going to fight C/F with everything I had. Maybe, in the end, I wouldn't be able to prevent it from overcoming my body, but I could prevent it from capturing my spirit. I've fought hard against C/F," he continued, his voice anxious in his determination to make me understand. "I slept in a mist tent for years. I've taken pills and treatments, had I.V.'s at home and in the hospital, and done everything my doctors said. In spite of all that, my lungs are getting worse."

For an instant, tears glistened in his eyes, but he blinked them away and went on. "Maybe I'm losing the lung part of me to C/F; but so far it hasn't touched the Lee part. I'll admit that there've been times, especially when I'm coughing hard and my chest feels like it's on fire, that I've been discouraged and felt like giving up. But I haven't.

"Don't you see? Marching tonight is a lot like going to scout camp. Only then, it was the fear of what the other scouts would think. Now, it's the fear of getting sick. If I stop doing things because I'm afraid, whatever the reason, then C/F has won. I will have allowed fear to govern my life."

He laid back down on the tilt table, and mechanically I resumed clapping his chest, my throat too tight to speak. Minutes passed and then, swallowing hard, I replied, "I don't want fear to govern your life any more than you do, Lee. But there are different kinds of fear; and it's only common sense to heed those that keep us from doing something dangerous that we'll regret later."

"I'll never regret marching tonight, even if it puts me in the hospital," he insisted stubbornly. "It's something I have to do. I can't let C/F rule my life. Not yet, anyway."

We looked unhappily at each other. Outside, the rain came down in torrents.

"Maybe the rain will stop," I said hopefully.

"And if it doesn't?" he questioned.

"We'll see," I dodged. "But first, I'm going to ask you a question, and I want an honest, carefully-considered answer. Don't answer it right now, because I want you to think about it. Sometimes when we want to do something so much it hurts, yet in our heart we know it wouldn't be smart, we depend on someone in authority, such as a parent, to stop us. Is that what's happening here?"

He opened his mouth to answer, but I cut him off. "No, I want you to think about it."

"I'll think about it," he promised, "but I already know the answer."

The day dragged. I prayed the rain would stop or that Lee would call from practice and say he'd decided that participating wasn't worth the risk. Instead, the rain turned to sleet, and the phone remained silent. My mind spun this way and that. Suppose he were to march? Getting cold and wet didn't necessarily mean he'd get pneumonia. Still, what if he did? And what if this time the antibiotics didn't work, and we lost him? I would never forgive myself. On the other hand, if he didn't participate, would he start thinking of himself as an invalid and give up? If so, C/F would have won—not because of his fears, but because of mine. I prayed for guidance.

At noon, I received an unexpected call from a C/F mother who lived in another part of the state. At one time we had corresponded regularly; but after her nine-year-old daughter died, our correspondence had dwindled down to notes on Christmas cards.

She was calling from a gas station. She and her husband were on a tight schedule enroute to Portland, but she'd been thinking about me; and while her husband filled the tank she had decided to call. Wanting to catch up on her news, I started asking questions about her family, but she cut me off. "I'll try to call you again on our way home when I have more time," she said. "Right now, I want to hear about Lee and how he's doing."

I told her about Lee, the band competition, the rain, and my dilemma. She didn't reply immediately; and as the silence continued, I was painfully aware of how insignificant my concerns must sound in light of her tragic loss.

I was about to turn the conversation to her trip when she said, "You haven't asked me for advice, Karma, and I'm glad, because I wouldn't know what to tell you. However, I will say this: We had a similar situation with Gwen* during the spring of her fourth grade in school. It was in March or April, probably the last of April. Anyway, it was an unseasonably cold day and raining. Gwen's class was scheduled for an outdoor field trip, and she had talked about nothing else for weeks. Considering the foul weather, I thought the trip would be cancelled; but when I called the teacher, she said this was the only day the trip could be taken.

"Gwen was just recovering from an infection, and I was afraid the cold rain would make it worse so I kept her home. She was devastated, but I told her that there would be another field trip in the fall. The weather would be warmer then.

"As you know, that was the summer Gwen's C/F caught up with her and she died. She never had her field trip. I wish now I would have—" Her voice trailed off and then resolutely resumed.

---

*Name changed.

"But, of course, I didn't dream then that she'd never have another chance. On the other hand, I suppose if I'd have let her go, I'd be thinking now that was why we lost her. Still—" Once more her voice trailed off.

In the background, I heard a car's horn summoning her. Hurriedly she said, "I wish I knew what to tell you." Then, promising to write, she was gone. I hung up the phone slowly. Perhaps without realizing it, she had told me what I needed to hear.

Lee called a few minutes later to say he had thought over what I'd said about subconsciously depending on his dad and me to protect him from unwise choices. While that was true in some instances, it wasn't in this case. This was something he had to do.

The rain didn't stop, and the temperature kept dropping. But when Borah marched onto the field, Lee was in his place, long johns under his uniform, two heavy pairs of socks on his feet. From the stands, we watched him smartly execute the complicated routine. Then, with the freezing rain and wind pummeling his back, he planted his feet firmly on the turf of the Boise State football stadium and triumphantly raised his trumpet to his lips. There were hundreds on the field, but I saw only him. My tears mingled with the rain, and I fancied that somewhere little Gwen was smiling.

Now, perhaps in a movie, Lee would not have sustained so much as a sniffle from the experience. But this was the real world, and a few days later he was in the hospital with pneumonia. When I berated myself to Dr. Venning for letting him participate, he brushed it off with a disparaging wave of the hand. "The cold and rain didn't have anything to do with it," he said. "The culprit is pseudomonas. We beat it down, and it comes right back. He was headed into a flare-up before he ever marched. Maybe the weather brought it on a few days earlier, but that's all." I hoped he wasn't lying to protect my feelings. I never knew with Dr. Venning.

In the meantime, Lee was very ill. Dr. Venning called the C/F

Center in Seattle, Washington, and the doctors recommended a new antibiotic. I prayed it would work.

After two weeks in the hospital and with no end in sight, Lee was antsy and Dr. Venning issued him a three-hour pass to go home. Ironically, on the way back to the hospital, we overtook a bus loaded with Borah's band. They were on their way to the Boise State stadium to perform during a game at half-time. Lee's eyes followed it as it turned off into the stadium parking lot.

In a few minutes, he was in his hospital bed, the I.V. back in his arm. A few blocks away, the band marched smartly onto the field to the standing applause of admiring friends and family. I wondered if anyone noticed the empty spot in the trumpet section.

1979: Lee was a proud member of Borah High's marching band.

—1980—

As he matured, Lee confided in me less frequently; and, occasionally, I was lulled into thinking that all was well, when, in fact, hurts were festering. One of those hurts burst open one night late in February, when I reminded him to start his treatment early because of basketball practice.

"I'm not going anymore," he announced venomously. "I'm tired of going to practices and never playing in the games. Last year when the coach needed me, I was plenty good enough; but this year more guys turned out, and I sit on the bench. He always says that if we don't come to practice we can't play in the next game. I don't know who he thinks he's kidding. Why doesn't he come right out and say that he's going to play certain players whether they come to practice or not? The leftovers will get to play once in a while as substitutes—except, of course, for Belnap, who is destined to rot on the bench. At least he'd be honest!"

"Aren't you exaggerating a bit?" I asked, shocked by his anger. "Not everyone can play all the time. Even if you haven't played as much this year, you enjoy belonging to the team, don't you?"

"Obviously, you've never played sports and don't know how humiliating it is to be the only one to sit on the bench game after game," he answered scornfully and closed the subject by snapping open his algebra book.

Recalling the many times he'd played while sick or with pain intense enough to have benched a less determined boy, I felt certain that his love for the sport would overcome his hurt pride. However, practice time came and went, and he continued to sit at his desk studying, or at least pretending to do so. I hoped he wasn't going to allow anger and hurt feelings to deprive him of something he loved to do. But how does one get across to a seething teenager who feels wronged by, of all people, his coach, that quitting is not going to solve the problem? All I could do was hope that by the next practice he would be over his pique and back on the gym floor.

However, he continued to miss practices and games, and I had finally decided that he truly meant what he'd said about quitting when, without explanation, one evening he asked me to do his treatment early because he had basketball practice. I was dying to know what made him change his mind, but I didn't dare pry. I only hoped it was because he had matured enough to realize that belonging to a team means being there, even if it's only to warm a bench or encourage teammates.

In April, a member of our stake presidency asked Lee to speak in stake conference on "How my Family and Home Life Have Strengthened My Belief in God." He wrestled with it all week. He wrote, crossed out, rewrote, and generally had a miserable time. On the way to the stake center he was still agonizing over it, moaning that it was a dumb talk and he didn't know why they'd picked on him in the first place when they knew he couldn't give good talks.

On the stand, his lips moved silently as he rehearsed his remarks one last time; and sitting in the audience, I worried with him, my hands as cold and clammy as his. However, when it was his turn to speak, only a pale face and an occasional crack in his voice betrayed his anxiety.

Normally, I hide my feelings well in public, but that evening I didn't care who saw my tears as Lee stood at the pulpit in front of that huge congregation and expressed his gratitude to the Lord for preserving his life and to his family for the part they had played in his spiritual development. He thanked his father, his brothers, and those who had administered to him in times of sickness. He thanked the ward members and his friends for the many times they had fasted and prayed in his behalf. Then he bore a beautiful, humble testimony that he believed in God and knew that He answers our prayers. Sometimes He may not answer them the way we want or at the exact moment we want them answered, but He always answers them, and always in a way that is for our eternal good.

On the drive home, he said in a puzzled voice, "You know, I hardly gave any of the talk I'd prepared. When I stood up, it was like I needed to say something different, and the words came out of the air."

"Out of the air—or from the Holy Ghost?" his father suggested quietly.

Lee thought for a moment. "From the Holy Ghost," he agreed.

Lee had a big seventeenth birthday. In the afternoon, his friend, Reed Nokleby, lured him away from the house while his friends gathered for a surprise party. The surprise was complete. Initially, he acted a bit stiff because he disliked surprises, but soon he recovered and had a grand time. After making short work of the birthday cake and ice cream, the guests scattered to get ready for the prom that night. Most of the boys, including Lee, had dates with girls who attended the party.

The prom was a perfect ending for Lee's birthday. Reporting in later that night, he stood at the foot of our bed, eyes gleaming. His date had looked enchanting in her long dress, and they had had a good time. But I scarcely listened to his words for looking at him. Dressed in a tux that complemented his broad shoulders and narrow hips, he looked so mature that my breath caught. Lee was rapidly turning from an awkward teenager into a handsome young man.

The three public high schools in Boise take turns sending their bands on an annual super activity. The year Lee was a senior, it was Borah's turn; they were invited to march during half-time at a Los Angeles Rams game during Thanksgiving vacation. For weeks, Lee was hip deep in band practices and fund-raising events. Often, he was out until eleven o'clock at night. By the time we finished his treatment, it was midnight before he could crawl into bed. Up again at 5:00 a.m. to get morning drainage in before another practice, he was averaging only five hours of sleep a night—not the best thing in the world for someone with C/F. But when I fussed at him, he said he was okay and not to worry.

Lee's excitement about the trip was contagious, and soon Dr. Venning was caught up in it, too. He listened to Lee's lungs and took blood tests twice a week in order to catch the first hint of an infection. In the meantime, I scurried around to find someone to help Lee with his treatments and find a way to pack a compressor, nebulizer, percussor, countless bottles of medicines, and necessary clothing into the one suitcase he was allowed to take.

I was almost to my wit's end when Emily Jasperson came to our rescue. She was accompanying the band as a combination nurse/chaperon and offered to help him with his drainages. Furthermore, she and her husband would take Lee's equipment suitcase with them. When I tried to thank her, she said it was nothing. Getting up an hour earlier and going to bed an hour later when you're worn out from chaperoning high-spirited high school students was nothing! I knew better than that, and I was grateful.

The day before Thanksgiving, Lee and about 280 other shouting, shoving band members boarded seven buses for their trip. Their itinerary was staggering. Although it included fun things such as a visit to Universal Studios, dinner on the Queen Mary, and a chance to play in the ocean for a few hours at Huntington Beach, it was far from all play. Besides the half-time show, they would march in several parades.

Sunday would be their toughest day. Immediately following their performance at the Los Angeles Rams' game, they would rush to the Hollywood Celebrity Christmas Parade, where they would participate in a long, grueling march. Naturally, I was concerned and tried to drill into Lee that there was no dishonor in using good judgment and stepping out of the parade rather than continuing on and getting into trouble. However, I knew even as I spoke that, in his eyes, anything less than finishing in grand style would be a personal defeat.

Lee was dead tired when he stepped off the bus on his return, but his eyes were glowing. The minute we were in the car, he burst out, "I made it! I marched the whole five miles of the Christmas parade. Some of the kids dropped out, and several times I thought I'd have to, too. But every time I was ready to quit, I said to myself, 'Take it a step at a time, and a note at a time, and you'll make it.' And I did!"

When I asked him about treatments, he said that no matter how early the wake-up call or how late they were out, Mrs. Jasperson was waiting for him. The other three boys in the room may have wondered where he slipped off to mornings before they were up and nights after they were in bed, but they hadn't asked. "Maybe they thought I was seeing a girl," he suggested hopefully.

—1981—

As the school year wound down toward the end of May, I devoted several evenings to typing term papers for Lee. He claimed he received higher grades when they were typed, and he was an agonizingly slow typist. I was on the last page of his economics paper, happily contemplating a cup of hot chocolate before collapsing into bed, when he tossed still another paper beside me. I smothered a groan, and he hastily assured me, "This one doesn't need typing. It's a psychology paper the teacher handed back today. It's pretty dumb, but you can read it if you want. We were supposed to write on who we are and how we feel about ourselves. He promised not to grade them or let anyone else read them. Like I said, mine is dumb. You probably won't want to read it." He started picking up the pages, suddenly embarrassed to have his mother privy to his feelings.

"I'd like to read it," I assured him, "unless, of course, it makes you uncomfortable."

He hesitated, torn between the child inside who wanted to confide in his mother and the young adult who treasured his privacy. "Well, you can read it, if you want," he finally conceded. "But after you read it, let it be. No rehashing! Okay?" I promised, and he handed me the handwritten sheets of paper and escaped to his room.

The first five pages could have been written by any high school senior struggling to answer the question, "Who Am I?" There were the usual superficial likes and dislikes when it came to clothes, music, television shows, friends, and so forth. On the sixth page, however, his writing changed abruptly, as if he had taken a deep breath and decided to tell it like it was.

He wrote: "There is another side to my life. I have a fatal disease called cystic fibrosis. It causes reduced lung capacity, but I've tried to overcome the handicap by trying harder in everything, from band to sports.

"I have been on medicine and in and out of hospitals since I was born. I have so much scar tissue from blood tests that the nurses have a hard time drawing my blood. I have gone to school with an I.V. needle in my arm for weeks at a time. When the dosage of medicine gets too large for I.V.'s at home, I'm put in the hospital.

"My kidneys have failed, my lungs have collapsed, I average pneumonia at least two or three times a school year. I am never completely well. I take pills every day with meals and antibiotics most of the time.

"I have seen five good friends die from C/F. They all died within two years of each other. The life expectancy is eighteen, but that's not realistic. Most of us die sooner. However, I don't plan my life around being sick or dying. I plan it around a long, full life. I'm going to fight to the end. I love life too much to quit."

After finishing the paper, I sat quietly staring down at it. It was only when a tear smudged the last page that I realized I was crying.

In May, Lee accomplished two of his goals. He graduated from the LDS seminary program and from high school. Watching him accept his seminary diploma, I thought of the hundreds of times he had sat up coughing all night and still forced his exhausted body up at 5:00 a.m. to get his treatment in before his early morning seminary class. No one would have faulted him for missing seminary those mornings, but that wasn't Lee's way. He only missed when he was in the hospital. Even then, he kept up with his written assignments. What a testimony of tenacity!

Two evenings after seminary graduation, he strode across the stand (how handsome he looked in his cap and gown!) and accepted his high school graduation diploma. I wanted to leap to my feet and give him a standing ovation; but instead, I sat quietly holding Kay's hand, blinking hard to keep back the tears.

Lee received many cards of congratulations, but the person who summed it up best was Dr. Venning, who wrote, "No one knows, except your parents, you, and I, what an achievement this is. Your faith will—as in the past—cause miracles to happen."

When I came home for lunch a few weeks later, Lee was plowing madly through his closet. His Sunday suit lay flung on the bed, and his hair was glistening from the shower.

"What in the world . . . ?" I exclaimed. He cut me off.

"Gladys Wilson died," he said, his voice squeaking with tension. "Her family found a note among her papers saying that when she died she wanted Brother Dixon to conduct a graveside service and me to speak. They must have just found the note or something, I don't know. Anyway, Bishop Thurber called me this morning. He's going to pick me up in a minute and take me to the cemetery." He continued rifling through his closet. "Don't I have a clean white shirt?" he wailed, knocking clothes off their hangers in his haste. "And look at my dress shoes! Will you polish them for me?"

I reached past him and pulled out a clean white shirt while I tried to digest what he was saying. My son, who had never attended a graveside service, was going to speak at one? Grabbing shoes and polish, I asked hopefully, "You have in mind what you're going to say, I suppose?"

"Kinda. I wish you or Dad had been here to give me some pointers, but I've jotted down a few things. That's why I'm late getting ready. Will there be a pulpit to put notes on?"

"Not at a graveside service. Maybe you can cup them in your hand," I replied, still finding it difficult to picture my reticent son delivering a eulogy.

While rubbing polish on his shoes, I thought about Gladys Wilson. We were not well acquainted, but we shared a common love for literature and visited occasionally by phone. She was a member of our ward, but seldom attended, preferring to stay home and read and write during her spare time. Lee and LaMar Dixon were her home teachers, and until a few months ago when she had become ill and moved away, they had visited her every month. She was probably better acquainted with them than anyone else in the ward. Still, with all the polished speakers available, I was surprised that she had chosen Lee to speak at her service.

Handing him his shined shoes, I offered, "Why don't I call the office and make arrangements to go with you?"

"No, thanks," he replied, trying not to sound ungracious. "No offense intended, but I would be even more nervous then." A car horn sounded. He gave me a quick peck on the cheek and tore out the door, buttoning his suit coat as he went. I watched the car pull away, hoping he had remembered his notes.

I rushed home after work, anxious to know how he had fared. "Well, I'd thought out a two-minute talk," he said, "but when the time came to give it, I forgot half of what I was going to say. Still, overall, I did pretty good. In fact, personally, I think I did a great job."

I thought to myself, "He prepared a two-minute talk and forgot half of it! That's got to set a new record for brevity."

"Actually," he reflected, "I didn't really know Sister Wilson that well, but she was a nice lady. I guess Brother Dixon and I were about her only visitors, except for family. I'm surprised that she thought enough of me to ask that I talk; but, now that it's over, I'm glad she did. She may even have chosen me because she knew I didn't talk much, and she didn't want a long, drawn-out service."

"In that case, she made a perfect choice," I thought.

On the last day of August, Lee started college at Boise State University. However, within the month he was back in the hospital with pneumonia. He was admitted to the same room he'd occupied during his last stay; and, sitting beside him, it seemed to me as if the intervening months had never existed. The squeaking wheel on the medicine cart as it made its rounds, the squawking intercom system, the hospital smells, the swaying I.V.

tube, the blue lips and fingernails, the gray, drawn face and grinding cough—nothing had changed, not even the icy fear that knotted my stomach and made my hands tremble.

Quietly, so as not to disturb Lee, I rose from my chair and searched in the hospital closet for a blanket, knowing even as I reached for it that it didn't matter how many I huddled under, the coldness inside me wouldn't thaw until he was safely home. Perceptively, he opened his eyes and said, "Not to worry, Mom. Dr. Venning says I'm going to be okay." I forced a smile and gave him a thumbs-up sign.

While he was in the hospital, Lee had a surprise visitor. Lorraine*, a young married C/F friend in the advanced stages of C/F, was also in the hospital. When she discovered that Lee was two floors down, she wanted to see him. This presented a problem, because patients were not allowed to leave their own floor. Not to be deterred, she dressed in her street clothes and crept undetected out of her room and down the hall to the elevator. Reaching his room, she collapsed into the nearest chair. Although exhausted, she was, nevertheless, inordinately pleased with her achievement. Completely oxygen dependent, she dared stay only a few minutes, but that was long enough. She had done what she had come to do.

Fearing that she might collapse before she made it back, Lee rang her room until she answered and weakly assured him that she was fine. Telling me about it, he was torn between admiration for her "guts" and disbelief that she could be such an "airhead" as to leave her oxygen.

That night, after leaving Lee, I went up to fourth floor to look in on Lorraine. She greeted me with a wave of the hand, but she was coughing too violently to speak. I wondered how she had ever made it down to see Lee. Her husband, lying on the bed beside her, cradled her emaciated body in his arms. His face was white and anxious, but he said cheerfully, "She's getting out of here tomorrow. Her mother is flying in tonight to stay with us until she feels better."

---

*Name changed.

As I turned to leave, Lorraine whispered, "Tell Lee goodbye for me in case I don't see him before I leave tomorrow."

Lee was silent for a few moments after I gave him her message. Then he said slowly, "She's going home to die, isn't she? That's why she came to see me. She came to say goodbye, and I was so worried about her being without oxygen that I didn't figure it out." He reached for the phone. As I left the room, I heard him say, "Hi, Lorraine. This is Lee. Mom told me you're going home tomorrow, and I just want to say thanks for your visit and to tell you goodbye before you leave." His voice was steady. There were no tears. Those would come later during the sleepless night.

Ten days later, Dr. Venning discharged him to finish his meds at home. Shortly after his discharge, Lee found a part-time job working for the National Revenue Corporation as a telephone bill collector. It wouldn't have been my first choice for a job, but he was delighted to be making his own spending money. However, his job did complicate our already complicated lives. Now we had to juggle his meds and drainages around my job, his job, school, and church and sports activities.

Except for special dances, Lee's social life had consisted more of group activities than pairing off as couples. However, when he started college, that began to change. Especially after he met Jana.*

He recorded in his journal, "It's November 23, and I've taken Jana out for nearly two months now, and I'm starting to like her more and more. I don't want to tell her about my C/F for fear it will split us up. Sooner or later, though, I'll have to."

Another entry on December 24 reads: "Christmas Eve, and it's snowing. It's not a pleasant Christmas. I pulled the tendons in my shoulder playing basketball, and I have to keep my arm in a sling for a week or so. It hurts, but the worst thing is I had to cancel my date with Jana. I got her a little necklace, but I can't give it to her until after Christmas because I can't drive yet. Boy, I sure like her. I don't know how to tell her I have C/F. Hope it doesn't make a difference."

---

*Name changed.

—1982—

A month later, there was another entry in Lee's journal: "I guess Jana and I are over now. I don't know exactly what happened. Maybe someone told her I had C/F. Anyway, it was fun while it lasted."

As time passed, Lee became more independent about his health care, and this sometimes led to confrontations. In February, his pseudomonas bug flared into pneumonia, and Dr. Venning put him back on I.V.'s and told him not to attend classes for at least a week. However, instead of coming home from the doctor's office, he drove to the university where he took an exam, and then stayed for the remainder of his classes. When I jumped on him, he said he had finals scheduled for the rest of the week and had no intention of missing them. He reminded me that he was eighteen, had lived with C/F all his life, and had enough smarts to know when he was too sick to go to class and when he wasn't. "If I miss classes every time you and Dr. Venning get paranoid, I'll end up not graduating," he said angrily.

"If you ignore your doctor's orders and end up dead, you won't graduate, either," I retorted. On that unhappy note, he slammed upstairs to his room to study for the next day's exam while I washed the dinner dishes. From his bedroom came the sound of vicious, debilitating coughing.

When Dr. Venning called two days later, he sounded as if he was thinking aloud rather than talking to me. "I don't understand it," he mused. "Lee's white count and sed rate are higher today than a week ago; yet judging by the x-rays, the pneumonia hasn't infiltrated into any new areas. He doesn't get worse, but he doesn't get better either."

Feeling like a traitor, I asked, "Did he tell you he's been

attending classes all week?"

Dr. Venning grunted. "He told me. I said it was good for him—keeps his mind occupied and gives him some exercise."

I threw up my hands. How could he be so emphatic about something one day and completely change his mind the next? Lee was right. I should "butt out," as he had inelegantly put it, and let him work things out with his doctor. I resolved to do just that. And once or twice over the years, I almost succeeded!

As each of his older brothers left for a mission, Lee's desire to go intensified, and a few months before his nineteenth birthday he met with his bishop and his stake president. He wrote in his journal: "I had an interview about going on a mission with Bishop Thurber and President Ipsen, and they both say not to count on it. I am not, as of now, but it would be nice just to try. Even if I get sick a week after I leave, I'd like to try. If I cannot go, I'll try not to be too disappointed. I don't say anything, but I live with disappointments all the time."

A few weeks later, Lee met again with his bishop. I suspect that he had already prepared himself for a negative answer. Still, I could tell it hurt when his bishop told him that, because of his health, he would not be called, at least at this time.

During the months that followed, his friends left on their missions. He attended each of their farewells, smiling and wishing them well, carefully keeping to himself the hurt of being left behind. As for me, while I was sad that my son had to suffer this additional disappointment, paradoxically, I was relieved that he wasn't going. He was almost constantly on antibiotics now, and at least every six months he was hospitalized. How could he survive if he were caught in a situation where he couldn't receive the immediate kind of medical care he required? Yet, when I heard of other C/F boys fulfilling missions and doing well, I wondered if it all boiled down to a question of faith. Lee had the faith. But did Kay and I? I wasn't sure. I only knew I was grateful that the decision had not been ours to make.

During the year, Lee had become an excellent typist, and I was surprised when he asked me to type his English paper. When I got into the paper, however, I realized that he hadn't given it to me for my typing skills, but rather as an excuse to share his feelings. The assignment was to write a two-page article on death. The requirements were simple: the paper was to be typed and was not to reflect the writer's religious beliefs.

I was relieved that Lee holed up in his room and didn't watch my face as I typed his words:

"I may have thought about death more often than most young adults because I have cystic fibrosis, an incurable lung disease. I am considered one of the lucky ones to have survived this long. However, the attitude of 'it won't happen to me, just to other people' is not my attitude since I know that before long, it will happen to me. Therefore, quality of life, not length of life, is my measuring stick; and I am trying to make the time I have left productive time. My time is basically used for improvement of myself—be it spiritual, physical, or mental.

"Years ago, my doctor gave me a clipping which is thought to have been written by a young cystic fibrosis girl. I've tacked it to the bulletin board in my room, for it sums up my outlook on life:

> Some may feel I am fighting a losing battle, but I will not go down without the best fight I can possibly give. My family, friends, and self-respect have never allowed me to give up. I live each day as if it were my last. We are born for a reason: my goal is to be able to leave behind some little special something as a result of my life.

"Like the author of the above, my goal is to use whatever amount of time I have left productively, so that when my time comes to move on, I can go without regrets. To me, death is not wanted, yet it is not to be feared, for I do not believe that death is the end of existence."

I read those words, written by my nineteen-year-old son—a young man on the threshold of life, one who loved life so very much and yet lived each day knowing that disease was methodically destroying his body—and I wondered again at his great courage.

As Lee went through his teens, it was difficult for him to tell us in so many words that he loved us. He didn't want to be "mushy." But in our family testimonial meeting during our August reunion, he stood and tearfully expressed his love for his family. He later recorded in his journal, "The family reunion last week was fun with water skiing, boating, and eating. The whole family was there, somewhere around twenty-five of us. That's a huge crowd for the cabin. We had a special family meeting on Sunday, and those who wanted to expressed their love for the Lord and for each other. It was the first time I have cried without physical pain to cause it. I felt like a baby, but I also felt grown-up to be able to cry because of the love I feel for my family."

Near the end of August, Lee was back in the hospital with pneumonia, and I was faced with the wrenching decision of whether to attend Steve's graduation from BYU or stay with Lee. Neither decision felt right.

It was Lee who brought up the subject. "When you get to Provo tomorrow," he instructed, "tell Steve I tried to stay well long enough to watch him graduate, but I couldn't quite make it."

"I haven't decided yet whether or not I'm going," I replied as casually as I could manage, "but if I don't go, Dad will tell him."

He stared at me, incredulous. "Why aren't you going?" he demanded. Before I could speak, he answered his own question. "It's because I'm in the hospital, isn't it?" Again, he didn't wait for my reply. "Mom," he cried passionately, "I'm going to be in and out of hospitals all the time now, but Steve is only going to graduate this once. I want you to go. It isn't like I'm real sick or anything."

We were interrupted at that point by Dr. Venning, checking on Lee one last time before he left for the night. He told us that he had sent a sample of his blood to a lab in California and would continue sending them samples three times a week. He didn't want any surprises from the new medication he'd prescribed. Feeling the glands in Lee's neck, he said casually, "Lee tells me that Steve is graduating from college, and you and your husband are going down to his graduation. Give him my best wishes." When I didn't respond, he must have guessed that I didn't feel comfortable leaving Lee because he added, "Lee will be in here for at least another week before we let him finish his meds at home. He'll be fine while you're gone."

After a sleepless night, I arose early and packed my suitcase, still not having made a firm decision. We would be stopping at the hospital on our way out of town, and I would make it then. If Lee looked better, I'd go. If not, Kay would go without me. I knew Steve would understand.

At the hospital, Lee said he was feeling better. But his gray, pinched face and dusky lips and nails belied his words, and I told him that I wasn't going. He dropped his eyes and pleated the sheet between his thin fingers. "Steve will be disappointed if you and Dad aren't both there, Mom. This is a big day for him. I don't want to make you miss it."

"You're not making me miss it," I interrupted. "I'm staying because it's what I want to do."

"You're staying because I'm in the hospital," he responded. "But I'll be okay without—" A vicious coughing spell made it impossible for him to continue, and he shot his dad an imploring look.

Kay took me by the elbow and propelled me to the corner of the room. "Karma," he whispered, "don't dump a load of guilt on him."

"What do you mean?" I protested, jerking my arm away. "I'm not dumping guilt on anyone. He's sick, and I'm not going to leave him."

"Exactly. You're not going to Steve's graduation because he's sick. How do you think that makes him feel? He's got enough problems without adding guilt to them."

I opened my mouth to protest, and then closed it. I knew he was right. Yet, with C/F, complications can develop in an instant. If something happened while I was gone, I'd never get over it.

I looked at Lee, and our eyes met. I walked over, kissed him goodbye, and blindly left the room.

When we arrived back in Boise, I insisted on going straight to the hospital from the freeway. Lee had improved while we were gone, and he was anxious to hear about Steve's graduation. He smiled and said I was prejudiced when I told him that Steve was the best-looking graduate there, and laughed aloud when I related how he had dozed off during one of the speeches and almost slipped out of his chair because he'd worked from 11:00 p.m. the night before until 7:00 a.m. that morning. I filled him in on the fun we'd had with Stan and Pat and their families, and gave him the cards and messages they'd given me to deliver. Concluding, I said, "It was a wonderful two and a half days, and I'm happy you talked me into going."

He smiled at that and returned smugly, "I told you I'd be fine. You worry too much!"

In November, Lee received his endowments in the Provo Temple. He had realized another of his goals, and this one was the most important of all.

—1983—

Monday, February 7, 1983—Entry from Lee's Journal:

"I have decided to give Brigham Young University a try, come fall. I think I would enjoy myself more down there and have more fun. Boise State is a good school, but the social life isn't here. BYU seems more of a place to go to have fun and *find a wife.* Hopefully, I can live with Roger so he can help with my drainages. I told Mom tonight. I could tell it scared her, but I know she'll support me in it."

Actually, Lee left home earlier than he had anticipated. Just before the semester ended at BSU, Pat called him. She and Robert owned a combination convenience store and service station in Orem, Utah, and one of their employees was leaving. Would Lee be interested in living with them and working at the Quick Stop as clerk and bookkeeper when school was out? Of course, he was delighted. I was unstrung.

Lee considered Dr. Venning his friend as well as his doctor, and before he left for Orem he drove to his office to say goodbye. Although it was a social call, Dr. Venning pulled out his stethoscope for one last listen to his lungs. As Lee left, he gave his shoulder a squeeze and said huskily, "You're going to be all right down there, boy."

Pat found a doctor in Orem whose practice included several C/F young adults, and Dr. Venning mailed him Lee's medical records. He sent me a copy of the letter he had enclosed. In part, he had written: "I am writing you a brief note about my friend and patient, Lee Belnap. I have been Lee's physician since he was eight weeks of age, at which time he had severe cystic fibrosis with pneumonia. Lee is a very quiet, reserved personality, with unlimited courage and an inspiration to all of us who have worked with him.

"I have so many record notes on this boy that it fills more than two files. I am merely going to send you the most recent facts about his continual, courageous fight with his illness. Take special care of him."

It was a tradition in our family to honor the child who was spreading his or her wings for the first time with a special dinner and an evening of favorite stories about the honoree. This time it was Lee's turn to be honored. Emotions were near the surface, and we deliberately kept the tales funny. However, when Kay gave him a special father's blessing, eyes overflowed. The grandchildren, disturbed by adult tears, asked why we were crying. Why, indeed? From the time he was small, Lee's driving ambition had been to rise above C/F and to live a full, productive life. This was a major step toward that goal. Why, then, were there tears?

Early the next morning, Lee kissed us goodbye. Kay and I stood on the porch and waved until his car turned the curve and drove out of sight. Then we turned, put our arms around each other, and walked into our empty home. For once, hurrying off to work was a relief.

That night Pat called. Lee had arrived safely and had already had a couple of drainages. Then, in a little girl's voice she said, "Mom, I'm scared. I didn't think about the responsibility I was taking on when I asked Lee to come. You made caring for him so natural when I lived at home that I didn't think it was any big deal. But tonight during his treatment, he coughed so hard he almost threw up. After he caught his breath, I asked him if he was okay, and he shrugged and said that's the way he is now. It hit me then that I'm responsible for him, and I saw him through new eyes. For all his bravado, he's really living on the edge, isn't he? What if I make a mistake and he gets really sick down here? I feel so responsible." Her voice quivered, and I knew she was trying not to cry.

My heart went out to my tender-hearted daughter. The one

thing I had never intended was for Lee's brothers and sisters to feel responsible for him. I wanted them to love and enjoy him, and yes, even look after him, but only in the same brotherly and sisterly manner they looked after each other. In other words, I wanted them to be involved in his life, but not burdened by it. Sometimes the line between the two, like now, was thin.

"Patty," I said, unconsciously reverting to her childhood nick-name, "Lee may very well get sick while he's down there. But it won't be because of anything you do or don't do. As you know, he gets sick here, too. It's the disease—as Dr. Venning reminds me when I berate myself for something I've done or not done. You must remember, too, that Lee isn't a little boy like he was when you left for college. He's twenty years old and knows how to care for himself. He's a self-disciplined and responsible young man."

"But what if he gets really sick down here?" she persisted.

"Then he'll either check in with Dr. Lewis or the C/F Clinic in Salt Lake. If it turns out to be serious, Dad and I can be there within hours of your call. Or Lee can catch the first flight home." We talked for a few more minutes, and she sounded more sure of herself when she hung up.

In spite of my brave words, I was nervous, not only for Lee but for Pat. She was a conscientious, sensitive girl, and I knew if Lee's health took a turn for the worse while he was with her, she would never get over it. On the other hand, Lee would be crushed if I asked him to come home. I prayed that Lee would stay well, and that it would be a delightful summer for all of them.

Unable to sleep, I wandered through the house, ending up in Lee's room. Surveying the too-tidy room, twenty years of memories flooded over me—happy memories of bright, wonderful days when we could almost forget he had C/F, and fearful memories of dark nights when we wondered if dawn would ever come. Conversations came to mind—cheerful ones filled with dreams for a glowing future, and gut-level ones about digging down deep and holding on when there appeared to be no future. I looked at his picture, smiling at me from his dresser, and whispered to him, "I've tried to teach you to trust in the Lord and live with courage and optimism, my son. Now I must learn to do the same."

Lee did stay well, and he spent a busy and fun summer with Pat, Robert, and their children. It was a time his older nieces and nephews would always remember.

In the fall, Lee moved to Provo to begin school at Brigham Young University. After settling in, he wrote, "We are moved into our apartment on campus. It isn't bad, but needs fixing. There are four of us, and Roger and I room together. I'm enjoying BYU and am glad I decided to take a chance and come here. Our ward is an older ward, not too many cuties; but the bishop is a real cool guy. Therapy is going fine. We do it around 7:00 in the morning, then around 6:00 after dinner. I'm cooking for myself, and I'm even eating more and better than at Pat's—if that's possible. Not to worry, my health and finances are both good."

In a later letter he wrote, "My health is fine, but you need to counsel Roger! Two minor wrecks and the artificial joint in his elbow (result of a high school injury) replaced, all in one semester! I don't know about that boy! Until his arm isn't so sore, I'm doing my own back and getting along okay.

"Last Saturday Darrell, one of our roommates, and I took off for the day. We went up to Solitude and then hiked into a place called Silver Lake which was beautiful. On the way back to Salt Lake, we took an off-road toward Guardsmen Pass, and at the top we left the car and hiked up to the summit.

"The hike in the high altitude made me so short of breath, I thought I was going to die; but the view was spectacular. We could see Park City, Heber, and the next mountain range which was probably a couple hundred miles away. God created a beautiful world for us to live in. Life is good!"

—1984—

Wednesday, January 11, 1984—Entry from Lee's Journal:

"I spent three weeks at home and had a peaceful, relaxing, fun rest—a most pleasant vacation. The whole family was home for Christmas. Holidays are sure great, getting together and seeing the family. We are a close family, and I'm glad.

"I paid Dr. Venning a quick social visit while I was home, and he said he plans to retire in June because of his health. That was shocking news.

"I still plan on graduating in April '85. It will be exactly four school years since I started college. I'm proud of myself for making it in four years with good grades. I have proved a lot of things to myself."

Lee sailed through his year at BYU in remarkably good health until the week before he was to leave for home. Then the pseudomonas bug flared. Buried in writing term papers and taking finals, he told himself it was merely a cold and that he'd see Dr. Venning when he arrived home. Unfortunately, pseudomonas infections don't wait on term papers or final exams, and he became steadily worse. Somehow, he managed to tough it out, and the morning after his last final he headed for home. The drive home, he said, was a nightmare. In fact, when he reached Salt Lake, he was so short of breath and had such a throbbing pseudomonas headache that he swung off the freeway and drove to the C/F Clinic, where the doctor listened to his lungs and ordered an x-ray and a pulmonary function test. He suggested that Lee check into the hospital for a few days, but Lee had convinced himself that he had a plug rather than pneumonia and asked for a treatment instead. During the drainage, he coughed up a cup of dark, thick mucus and felt much better. However, a few miles out of Salt Lake, the headache and shortness of breath returned. When I asked why he hadn't turned back, he confessed, "I didn't want to be hospitalized down there. If I'm going to end up in the hospital, I'd rather be home."

The next morning, Dr. Venning examined him and prescribed medication for the pneumonia. Then, gripping Lee's shoulder, he said briskly, "Good to have you home, boy. You're going to be fine." Lee grinned and nodded. The doctor picked up his three-legged stool, and humming to himself, disappeared down the hall to care for his next patient. We were back in familiar territory.

But not for long. In June Dr. Venning retired, and Lee's medical records were transferred to Dr. David Merrick, the lung specialist who had assisted in the Nampa/Boise C/F Clinic for many years and was well acquainted with Lee. He was a competent, caring physician; but there was only one Dr. Venning, and Lee and I had tears in our eyes when we walked out of his office for the final time.

A few weeks later, Kay scared us nearly witless. I had only been at the office for an hour when Lee called and said something was wrong with his dad and that I needed to come home. Thinking heart attack or stroke, I told him to call an ambulance, but he was certain it was neither of those. Seconds after I arrived home, I realized that Kay didn't know who I was. Not only was his memory gone, but he couldn't remember what was happening from one minute to the next. The diagnosis at the hospital was transient global amnesia.

As the day progressed, Kay's memory slowly returned. By evening, the only blank spot was from the night before, when he'd been reading in bed, to that afternoon, when he found himself in a hospital bed surrounded by his family staring down at him with frightened eyes.

On the way home, Lee sat tensely in his seat, eyes staring straight ahead. Finally he said, "I think Dad not remembering me this morning was the awfulest thing that's ever happened to me." He paused and then asked in a strained voice, "When I die, you won't forget me, will you, Mom?"

Silently, I shook my head. I couldn't speak for the lump in my throat.

Wednesday, August 15, 1984—Entry from Lee's Journal:

"A lot of time has passed since my last journal entry, and many things have transpired. Steve married Kristy Rigby in the Salt Lake Temple on July 30, and we had an open house in our yard for them a few days later. The K & K [Karma and Kay] Connection used it as an excuse to redecorate the house, paint the fence, and plant flowers all over. I did more work than I can write.

"Besides working, I played softball on the church senior team with Steve and coached the Joplin Elementary School fifth grade girls' team. Two of my nieces, Marcie and Angie, were on the team. I really enjoyed the 'Crazy Cosmos' and hope they had a fun time. I think I did pretty well to take the girls from knowing nothing to a fourth place team!

"As I write this, I'm at the cabin in McCall with Dad and Mom. We've been here a week. I've gone water skiing every morning, but mostly I have enjoyed taking life easy, getting my mind and body ready for school. I will be leaving for BYU in about three weeks, and Roger and I will room together again at Raintree. I hope my health stays the way it has. I'm surprised at how well I'm staying.

"Dr. Venning retired in July. I will miss him. He really cared for me; nobody else can match the job he has done for me."

Thursday, September 6, 1984—Letter from Lee:

"Health-wise, all is fine with me. School-wise, not so fine. I, among others, was dropped from one of my prerequisite classes because they overbooked it. I won't be able to graduate until

August now. Bummer. However, I enjoy it here. The apartment is busy and noisy so I do my studying at the library. The ward is fun. A lot of cuties—rich, too! Thanks for a good summer. Love, Lee."

Two weeks after he wrote this letter, he phoned me at the office and announced that he had quit school. I was stunned. Only two nights before, he had called to tell us how well he was doing. With graduation only a year away and his health holding, his dream of graduating from BYU was rapidly becoming a reality.

Shocked into silence, I listened to his raging voice. Never before had I heard him so angry. He said that he had been assured when he was dropped from the prerequisite class that he could take it the next semester, and his graduation would only be delayed from April to August. He was disappointed, but he felt he could live with that. But now, not only was the class not being offered next semester, but the curriculum for his major was being changed. Because he was not presently taking the class, he would be subject to the new curriculum requirements. This meant it would take him at least two more years to graduate, perhaps longer.

"It's not fair," he said bitterly. "I registered early for that class, and it isn't my fault it was later overbooked. When they knew we had to take that class or be caught in the curriculum change, why didn't they add another class?"

"Perhaps, if you talked to them . . . ," I began.

He cut me off. "What do you think I've been doing for the past two days? They don't see what the big deal is. So it takes another year to graduate! So what? They act like all we have to do is go to school! I can't make them understand that I don't have that kind of time or that kind of money," he continued angrily. "If I'm going to be productive at all, I've got to graduate and get into the job market before my health crashes."

"Did you explain that to them?" I asked, unwilling to believe that there wasn't a mistake somewhere, and that once it was brought to the attention of the proper person, the situation would be remedied.

"Of course I did. I even swallowed my pride and told them I had C/F. Never thought I'd ever use that as a begging tool, but I did. It didn't make any difference. I doubt if they even know or care what C/F is. They talk a lot about caring for the individual; but when the chips are down, we're just a bunch of numbers. Anyway, I've quit, and I'm going to work at the Quick Stop for Pat and Robert for a year. Then I'll return to Boise and enroll at Boise State. I don't have time to waste on an extra year of school."

I knew this was not the time to point out that if he worked for a year before transferring to Boise State, he would still not graduate for two years—and possibly not then if he lost credits in the transfer. Time-wise, he would be as far along if he stayed at BYU. However, at the moment he was in no mood to listen to reason.

Lee was still sizzling when I called him the next morning, but he calmed down as we talked. I asked him why, if he was determined to quit at BYU, he didn't at least come home and start at Boise State now. Why work for a year? At that, his bitterness returned. "They said they won't refund my tuition money because it's past the withdrawal period. It doesn't matter that I didn't know earlier about the curriculum change," he said angrily. "Now I have to earn more tuition money."

"Lee, we'll pay your tuition," I interrupted. "You know that. Dad and I wish you'd stay at BYU, even if it takes two years to graduate. You've been happy there, and we wonder if you'll be content living at home and attending a smaller school now that you've lived on campus and had a taste of a larger university. I'm afraid you're letting disappointment and anger get the better of your good judgment. Promise me that you'll cool down and think about it." Reluctantly, he agreed.

Friday, September 28, 1984—Letter from Lee:

"Like I said on the phone, it's not because of the money that

I'm working. I know you will pay for my education. I just want to do it myself, and I enjoy the store. Right now I work from 4:00 p.m. until midnight. I do my therapy when I get up. By then everyone in the apartment has gone to school, and at midnight everyone is asleep, so I don't bother anyone."

Tuesday, October 30, 1984—Letter from Lee:

"A quick note. Even before your letter arrived, I had decided to go back to school next May. A calendar year is too long to wait. I mailed my admissions application to BSU and told BYU to mail my official transcripts, so I'm on my way.

"Health is good. Been eating well, not piecing at Quick Stop although I do drink more pop than normal. Not to worry, I'm okay."

Lee was best man at Steve's wedding reception.

—1985—

Monday, March 11, 1985—Entry from Lee's Journal:

"All in all, I feel good about coming to Utah. I proved to myself that I can live on my own and take care of myself. That was important to me. I've handled myself well in a difficult job and in difficult situations. I'm getting itchy, though, to get back to school and learn. I've decided to return home in May and go back to BSU and finish there.

"I missed two semesters of college, but I've gained insight into privately owned businesses. After working with Pat and Robert, I've decided I want to own and operate my own business. As of now, I would like a little soup, sandwich, and salad bar place in downtown Boise and call it, 'The Plate.' I'd line one wall with Dad's old license plates that are hanging in the garage. Get it? Sandwich plate—license plate! Maybe that's a dream, but it is my dream, however unlikely.

"I have also realized how important family is, and how much I want one. I have also seen how much the Church means, and the unhappiness that can be caused by deserting the Church.

"Roger and I are sharing a room together again at Raintree. He has been a good brother to me. If I had a choice of who I would room with out of all my roommates, this year and last, I would still pick Roger. This sums up my feelings."

On May 10, there were twenty-two candles for Lee to blow out. He was short of breath; but, luckily, his little nieces and nephews were willing "blowers," and no one noticed except me. Perhaps I wouldn't have been as aware had it not been that copies of two pulmonary function tests from the Salt Lake Clinic had arrived in the morning's mail. I quickly scanned through the first one until I reached the doctor's interpretation on the last page. He had written, "This degree of obstruction is consistent with end-stage cystic fibrosis."

End-stage cystic fibrosis! The words danced crazily on the page. It had to be a mistake! Lee hadn't been hospitalized for nearly three years. How could he be end-stage?

I looked at the date of the test and saw that it was dated a year earlier—April 20, 1984. The date rang a bell. That was the day Lee was so short of breath on his way home from Provo that he had stopped at the clinic, and the doctor had run a pulmonary function test. No wonder the results were terrible! Lee had taken the test when he was partially plugged off with pneumonia!

I looked at the date on the second test. It was taken less than a month before, when he was in Salt Lake for a checkup. He was well then, and the results would be much better. I flipped through the pages to the physician's comments, and my breath caught in my throat. I read, "Severe obstructive lung disease that has progressed since April 20, 1984. Consistent with end-stage cystic fibrosis." The first test results, then, had not been caused by a plug.

Somehow, I made it through the day. I even managed to laugh during the birthday party that evening. But inside, I was screaming, *Not end stage. Not yet. Not my Lee!*

After a sleepless night, I called Lee's doctor at the Salt Lake Clinic. He sounded rattled, and I knew that the test results must have been sent to me in error. However, after a few false starts, he explained that, although Lee had not experienced as many acute infections as formerly, his lungs had deteriorated into what is called "end stage cystic fibrosis." When I asked for his definition of "end stage," he retreated into technical jargon which I did not understand. He did say, however, that "end stage" didn't necessarily mean that death was imminent.

After hanging up the phone, I burned the reports, page by page, in the fireplace.

Following their graduation from BYU, Steve and Roger returned to Boise to work for Albertsons, Inc., Steve as an auditor and Roger as a computer programmer. They still enjoyed sports, and both boys played softball in the Albertsons employee softball league, with Steve playing for one of the more competitive teams and Roger for one that played "for fun."

The season ended with an all-day Saturday tournament, and Lee and I went down to watch. Both teams played well, and late in the afternoon they faced each other. Unfortunately, Roger's team had dwindled down until they were one player short; but, in spite of the automatic forfeit, they still wanted to play and looked around for a substitute. Roger volunteered Lee.

Lee declined, and I didn't blame him. The men on Steve's team were coming off a winning season. They might have already won the game by forfeit, but they would be playing for real. Of course, Roger's team would be delighted if they could pull off an upset, especially with a substitute player.

Thinking he had a graceful way out, Lee pointed out that he didn't have his softball shoes with him. Not to be thwarted, Steve dug through the trunk of his car and triumphantly produced an old pair of his. No matter that they were several sizes too large, they were regulation! With a muttered, "I'm going to make a fool of myself," Lee put on the shoes. And, indeed, his words did appear prophetic when he stumbled in the over-sized shoes and nearly fell. An audible groan went up from his team's supporters. Not only was the substitute a skinny kid who looked like he belonged in junior high, but he couldn't even walk onto the field without tripping over his own feet! It was obvious from his ramrod straight back that Lee had heard the groan. So had his brothers; and, as if on cue, they shouted from their respective benches, "You can do it, Lee!"

Lee pounded his fist into a borrowed mitt and hunkered down to play ball. For a few innings, the score stayed close, but then Roger's team went into a hitting drought while Steve's teammates placed their hits with deadly accuracy.

I don't know if it was the answer to my fervent prayers or because the opposing pitcher wasn't used to throwing to a batter of Lee's size, but Lee either singled or walked every time he came to bat. He didn't try for home runs or even a double; he just kept a keen eye on the ball and was content to get on base any way he could. He played the same way out in the field. There were no spectacular diving catches, just heads-up ball, constantly aware of where the runners were and where he needed to throw.

Steve's team won handily, but Lee's efforts did not go unappreciated. Surprised players on both teams sought him out and congratulated him on a good game. Driving home, the three boys talked about the game, punching each other and laughing. Watching them, I wished the moment could last forever.

As usual, there was much boating, water skiing, and eating at the family reunion in August. Lee took his turns, but I noticed that he didn't ski long or show off for his nieces and nephews. After jumping the wake a few times, he was content to just hold onto the rope and let the boat pull him over the water. I noted, too, that instead of joining in the general mayhem on the beach, he sought a chair in the shade. I asked him if the higher altitude was bothering him, and he shrugged and said, "A little." I suspected it was bothering him a lot.

In the evenings, the two of us slipped away early to do his drainage before the cabin was inundated with the rest of the family. Sometimes we talked, but most of the time we meandered through our own private thoughts, the stillness of the cabin broken only by the clapping of my hands and the occasional shouts and laughter drifting up from the beach. Once Lee asked me if I minded leaving the fun of the campfire to do his treatments. I answered truthfully that I wouldn't want to be anywhere else.

In October, we welcomed Paul Anderson into our family. He and Irene were married in the Boise LDS temple. All of our family were there, and it was a most glorious day.

When the C/F Foundation announced that the search for the C/F gene had been narrowed to 1/10 of 1% of the total DNA, a local TV station asked Lee for an interview. I was surprised that he consented. Although he didn't go to great lengths to conceal that he had C/F, he didn't wear it on his sleeve, either. Perhaps he agreed because he knew firsthand how frightening some C/F commercials and interviews can be to small C/F children, and just this once, he wanted to change that. At any rate, he asked that the interview be taped on Boise State's basketball court. There, in baggy sweats and a Boise State sweatshirt that camouflaged his thinness, he shot baskets (some three pointers!) while he explained the importance of the breakthrough.

When asked about his personal health and plans for the future, he cradled the basketball on his hip and looked directly into the camera. I had the feeling he was making a personal appeal to an unseen audience of C/F youngsters when he stressed the importance of beginning at an early age to assume responsibility, to follow the doctor's orders, and to never, never give up, regardless of how tough things were or what anyone said. As for his future—he was looking forward to a productive life.

That night, he watched the broadcast intently. When it finished airing, he said with a satisfied sigh, "That shouldn't scare any little C/F kid witless, now should it?"

A Belnap family reunion at McCall. Lee is at bottom center.

—1986—

Monday, June 16, 1986—Entry from Lee's Journal:

"I've always figured it would be C/F that would get me, but for a few seconds Saturday night I almost became a boating statistic—along with two of my friends.

"Roger and I had taken the boat to Lucky Peak Reservoir where we met some of our friends. We were almost ready to come home when I decided to take one last run. A friend, Scott Wolfley, was driving the boat when he was momentarily distracted, and the boat plowed into some large rocks at the base of a cliff. I saw the crash coming, but still barely had time to drop the rope and fling myself sideways before the boat hit a big boulder. I caught a glimpse of the boat going high in the air and tipping to one side as it went over the rocks. Then I couldn't see it anymore. I thought sure Scott and Paula had been killed. As it turned out, it somehow righted itself in the air before crashing into the water on the other side of the rocks.

"The crash wrecked the propeller and motor and ripped two big gashes in the bottom of the boat. Some boaters were close by and managed to tow it to shore before it sank. Then they came back to search for me. Scott was sure I had hit the rocks and was dead. Boy, was he relieved when he saw me bobbing in the water in my life jacket!

"Roger and his friends managed to get the boat onto the trailer and tow it home while I took Paula to the hospital for an x-ray. Ended up that her arm was bruised, but not broken.

"Although Dad isn't the yelling kind, I thought he might when he saw his boat, but he didn't say much. As for Mom, she kept saying, 'Forget about the boat. It's a miracle that your dad and I aren't standing on the shores of the reservoir right now while divers try to recover three dead bodies!' She gets pretty dramatic when she's upset.

"I feel real bad about the boat, but I can't express how overjoyed I was when I saw that Scott and Paula were okay. Scott called this morning and said that he thought his insurance would cover the boat. Hope so, because I doubt if ours will. But the bottom line is that I'm glad my friends and I are all in one piece."

Friday, December 19, 1986—Entry from Lee's Journal:

"Took my last college final today! Formal graduation exercises aren't until May; but I'm a full-fledged graduate of the College of Business with a Bachelor's Degree in Business Administration, with a major in Finance. Can you believe that?

"Now I need to get started being productive. I already have two job interviews set up for Monday. I should land one of them. I'm on my way at last!!"

The summer of 1986 was a great time for water-skiing.

—1987—

It never occurred to Lee that he would have a problem getting a job after graduation. He was a bright, well-disciplined, work-oriented young man and had much to offer an employer. But he also had cystic fibrosis. And, as a friend who worked as the personnel manager for a large corporation bluntly put it, "Lee would make an excellent employee, and I would take him in a minute if he didn't have C/F. But I can't justify hiring someone with a potentially fatal disease."

Week after week Lee searched for work, hounding employment agencies and pursuing the remotest of leads. He had risen above many disappointments in his life, but this one struck at his very core. Discouragement etched itself deeper into his face each time he returned from a fruitless interview. One night he said in a bitter tone, "I guess I should lie on the applications and say that I have perfect health instead of being honest. When they ask me about my C/F, I tell them it's under control, and it is. I haven't been hospitalized for over four years. I even offered to waive coverage under their medical plan if they were worried about their premiums going up."

In February his streak of good health broke, and he was hospitalized with pseudomonas pneumonia for two weeks. Three days after he was discharged, he insisted on taking the state personnel test. When I tried to talk him out of it, he argued, "I don't have a choice. The exam won't be offered again for several months. The private business sector isn't exactly standing in line to hire someone with C/F. Probably the state isn't either, but I have to give it a shot."

He was still on meds, and to conceal the catheter we maneuvered his arm through a long-sleeved shirt and put it in a sling.

Then I drove him to the exam site. When I picked him up three hours later, he eased himself into the car and rested his head against the back of the seat. He looked exhausted. "Boy," he exclaimed, "I didn't know how much this sick spell had taken out of me. I'm bushed." Then he cast me a smug smile. "I'm sure I did well on the exam, though. Now if someone will only hire me . . ."

In March, surrounded by family, Roger and Lori Stokes were married in the Boise LDS temple. All the children were married now except for Lee. That night during his treatment, he asked me if I was going to cry at his wedding. I told him that I always cry at weddings, and his would be no exception.

I was surprised when Lee wanted to go with me to our C/F chapter's annual spring conference. As it turned out, he was the only person with C/F present; the others were doctors, staff personnel, C/F parents, and volunteers.

Watching the physicians file in for the medical portion of the conference, I reflected on the change twenty years had wrought. Then, the medical meeting had overflowed with expectant parents, many having traveled hundreds of miles in the hope of learning something that would increase their child's chance for survival against a little-known disease. We had sat, pens poised over our yellow legal pads, asking dozens of questions, devouring every word the physicians uttered, and making copious notes to share with our doctors and the C/F parents back home. When researchers reported that progress was being made and there would be a future for our children, we snatched eagerly at this lifeline of hope. And if we didn't truly believe it would happen, at least we pretended to believe, for that was all we had.

This day's audience, in stark contrast, was few in numbers, and apathy rather than expectancy hung heavy in the room. A few doodled on their yellow legal pads; others stared vacantly at the doctors as they took their seats behind the long oak table. It was as if all hope had fled, and with it, the will to pretend.

Suffocating in the oppressive gloom, I looked around, hoping to see an animated face. In the back, I saw my friend, Lu. Two of her C/F children were dead now, and Karen, her third, was deteriorating rapidly. Feeling my glance, she attempted a smile, but her lips quivered; she quickly covered them with trembling fingers and looked away.

In the row behind me on the right sat a father and mother from another city. The mother's eyes were dark with hurt, and her husband grasped her hand tightly beneath the table. They had lost their second son to C/F only weeks before; but they had come anyway, hoping to bolster other parents. Perhaps later they could, but not this day. Their own wounds were too raw.

Across the aisle, I met the anguished eyes of still another mother. The day before she had called me from the hospital. Her daughter wasn't responding to the antibiotics, and she was frightened. I questioned her with my eyes; she shook her head and made a helpless gesture with her hands.

The moderator stood and introduced the panel of physicians. All except one were pediatricians from the Boise-Nampa areas with whom we were well acquainted. The other was from the University of Utah Medical Hospital and no stranger to those of us whose children were checked regularly at their C/F Clinic.

The meeting was short. The physicians recognized us as seasoned veterans of the disease and spoke to us as respected co-caregivers. They made no attempt to sugar-coat the facts or build up false expectations. The last speaker summed it up by saying, "Many of you present today have lost a child or children to this disease; many of you will still lose children. All we can say is to keep fighting. Progress, however slowly, is being made; and today's research, especially in the field of genetic engineering, will result in saving children tomorrow."

Anxious to escape this depressing atmosphere, Lee and I skipped the luncheon and fled to a nearby fast-food place where we indulged ourselves in a hamburger and milkshake. We talked about the upcoming baseball season, his new church calling as secretary to the stake mission president, and a promising job interview scheduled for the following week. We talked about everything except C/F.

In May, Steve, who had left Boise and was now working for Albertsons in Salt Lake City, leased the store portion of the Quick Stop from Robert and Pat and offered Lee a job. He would live with Steve and Kristy until he got his feet under him. It looked like an ideal situation. Steve needed a reliable person in the store, and Lee needed a job.

Lee had been in Utah less than a month when he called us. He managed to choke out that he was sick, and then a coughing spell forced him to surrender the phone to Steve. Steve had taken him to the Salt Lake Clinic that morning, and now he gave Kay and me the grim results. Lee's pulmonary function test showed a significant deterioration, and his exercise tolerance was "zilch." His arterial blood gases revealed severe room air hypoxemia (deficiency of oxygen reaching the tissues of the body). His doctor recommended hospitalization, but left it up to Lee as to whether it would be at the University of Utah Medical Center in Salt Lake or at St. Luke's in Boise. Whichever he chose, he must be admitted quickly.

Lee came back on the phone. In pain and racked with coughing, he said he'd decided on St. Luke's because once he was over the critical stage, I could give him his meds at home. That would mean a shorter hospital stay.

We drove Lee directly from the airport to the hospital, where he was immediately put on oxygen and started on intravenous antibiotics. That night he coughed up blood. The nurse assured us that it was not serious, but later when I passed her desk, I overheard her reporting it to Dr. Merrick. Complicating things still further, the doctor was almost certain that Lee had developed diabetes mellitus. This was not an uncommon occurrence in older C/F patients because of the involvement of the pancreas in the disease. They wouldn't know for a few days, but it looked like Lee could very well be oxygen and insulin dependent from then on.

Seeing his world shrinking around him, Lee was more despondent that night than I'd ever seen him. "If no one wanted to take a chance on hiring me when my health was decent," he remarked bitterly, "they certainly won't when I'm hooked up to an oxygen tank."

"Oxygen is still only a maybe," I emphasized, "and then possibly only at night." He grunted disparagingly.

Groping for the right words, I asked, "Lee, have you ever considered employment options other than working for someone else?"

"Like what?" he asked.

"Oh, I don't know. Maybe you could start your own bookkeeping business. Beginning professionals often hire someone outside their office to keep their books. That would give you flexible hours, and you could work around your C/F."

"Yeah, I suppose."

For a minute I thought he was placated, but then he burst out, "Working at home is for old, retired men who need something to fill their spare time. They've already had a career. I'm young. I want a real job with a real company. I want to compete and prove that I can hold my own in the business world. I'd do a good job, too," he continued. "I've done a good job managing the store at the Quick Stop for Steve. Just ask him." He paused, and his lips twisted. "Speaking of Steve," he said, his shoulders slumping, "you'd better call him tonight and tell him to look for a new manager. He can't work in Salt Lake and run the store in Orem without a manager, and I don't know when I'll get back there. If the doctor puts me on oxygen around the clock, I probably won't get back."

In the end, Dr. Merrick decided Lee wouldn't need oxygen after he left the hospital. Lee was relieved; I was concerned. His room air oxidation had only improved slightly from what it was when he was admitted to the hospital, and I was worried that the effort of breathing would damage his heart. As for the diabetes, they would try to control it by diet.

A week later, Steve and Kristy drove in from Salt Lake, bringing with them a business proposition for Lee. They were negotiating for a sandwich shop in Salt Lake, and they wanted Lee to manage it. If he wanted to accept a low salary, he could even use the difference between the low salary and a higher one to buy into the shop.

Lee's eyes sparkled at the possibility. I looked at him, short of breath even on oxygen, skinny as a scarecrow, hooked up to an I.V., and talking with Steve about managing and buying into a sandwich shop. It was insane; yet their excitement was contagious. After all, anything was possible, wasn't it?

Lee must have confided his plans to Dr. Merrick, because a few days later he told me that if the purchase of the shop depended on Lee managing it, he would recommend that Steve not purchase it. "Lee's condition has deteriorated considerably," he explained. "He's no longer climbing back after hospitalization, and realistically, we've got to expect him to be hospitalized more frequently and for longer periods of time. I don't expect him to be really well again, and certainly not well enough to hold down a full-time job. I feel he's jeopardizing his health to try."

That evening, listening to Lee's grandiose plans to manage and eventually own the sandwich shop, my heart grew heavier by the minute. Cautiously I said, "Your plans for the sandwich shop sound wonderful. But the way I see it, your major job right now is making certain that when the control for C/F comes—and it will come—your body will still be in decent shape. That may require making sacrifices now that you don't want to make."

"Such as?" Lee questioned.

"Such as twenty-four-hour-a-day oxygen if it becomes necessary to protect your heart, and—"

"And what?" he interrupted, anticipating what I was going to say.

I took a deep breath. "And putting full-time work on hold for a while, even if it means not working at the Quick Stop or managing a sandwich shop for Steve." It was said, and I waited.

Lee didn't answer immediately. Then he shook his head. "I'll do whatever it takes—oxygen, I.V.'s, insulin, whatever; but if Steve's purchase goes through, I'm going to work at the sandwich shop. If it doesn't materialize, I'll try to find work somewhere else. I hope you're right and a control will come, but I can't sit around, wasting what time I have left, hoping for something that may or may not happen. For as many months or years as I'm able, I'm going to be productive."

At the same time Lee's health was deteriorating, so was my husband's; on July 2 an angiogram showed that the arteries supplying blood to his kidneys were blocked, and he needed immediate surgery. Because of his heart condition, the surgeon was not optimistic. However, there were no other options, and he scheduled the operation for the following morning.

I drove home to give Lee a treatment, and as soon as it was finished he accompanied me back to the hospital. I'd walked possibly a quarter of a block from the parking lot when I realized I was walking by myself. Looking back, I saw Lee leaning against a parked car, struggling to get his breath. His face was gray. He admitted that he'd been short of breath and coughing hard all day. "Don't get so shaken up," he said as I questioned him. "It's only a plug, and it'll soon move or I'll cough it up and be fine. Come on, or Dad will wonder what's keeping us."

We went on, my gait slowed to his. We had just walked in when the surgeon came with consent papers for Kay to sign. While Kay read them, the doctor stole sidelong glances at Lee. I didn't blame him. His breathing was rapid and ragged, his color bad. Looking at father and son, the thought that I might lose both of them nearly destroyed me.

Kay's surgeon was beaming when he came into the waiting room the next day to tell us the operation had been a success. Barring complications, Kay would be off the critical list in a few days.

Lee, on the other hand, continued to get worse. He coughed constantly, and the disposable cup into which he coughed thick brown globs of mucus was never far from his hand. He rarely slept, and when he did, he moaned with each breath.

In the middle of September, Dr. Kane came from Salt Lake to our Nampa/Boise Clinic, and I took Lee to Nampa to be examined. After taking the usual tests, Dr. Kane motioned us into an adjoining room. "The chest x-ray shows severe hyperinflation and increased linear markings with pseudomonas pneumonia in both lungs," he said tersely to Lee. "Your pulmonary function test was crummy, and your weight has dropped to 101 pounds—and that's with those heavy boots on." Without mincing words, he told Lee that he was caught in the downward spiral common to advanced lung disease patients. He explained that repeated lung infections cause the loss of strength and body mass needed to fight off infections, which, in turn, allows additional lung infections.

The doctor stopped speaking for a minute and stared at us thoughtfully. When he resumed, it was to give Lee two options. The first was to continue with what he was doing—continuing the inhalation treatments, enzymes, diabetic diet, and I.V. therapy. The spiral would, however, continue, and down the road a few months his body would become too weak and the infections too massive for the drugs to overcome. At that point, it would be over.

The other option could buy him some time. When Lee asked how much, he shrugged. He didn't know; perhaps a few additional months, perhaps a few additional years. In any case, it would involve unpleasant procedures. Without elaborating on what those procedures were, he turned to me and asked, "Which will it be?"

Caught off guard by the abruptness of the question and that it was directed to me rather than to Lee, I fumbled for words. Finally I managed to say, "Lee knows my feelings; but this is a decision he has to make." The doctor shifted his eyes to Lee, and I closed mine, waiting for his answer.

Only a slight tremor in his voice betrayed his turmoil as he replied with forced lightness, "I still have things to do and places to see. So let's go for it."

"Good," Dr. Kane answered briskly. "I want to admit you into the hospital in Salt Lake early Monday morning, and this is what we're going to do—"

Quickly, he outlined the treatment. To combat the continuing weight loss, Lee would learn how to insert a tube through his nose into his stomach. This would enable him to receive an additional 1200 calories of nutrients through nighttime feedings while he slept. He would begin steroids to increase his body mass, and would switch to a new pancreatic enzyme to help him digest his food more efficiently.

Dr. Kane pointed out that since the effort of breathing burned up more calories than Lee was able to consume, it was important that he be on oxygen. Perhaps, once the pneumonia was under control, he would only need it during the night; but at least for the present, he would be on it twenty-four hours a day. As for the pneumonia, he would institute a three-week course of antibiotics intravenously beginning Monday morning. Since Lee would now be on meds more frequently and for longer periods of time, he recommended that a central line be implanted in a vein in his arm to run directly to his heart. Not only could it be more easily accessed, but it would save wear and tear on his fragile veins.

The short trip home from Nampa seemed endless. The doctor's words pulsated in my brain, making me physically ill. Not wanting Lee to see my trembling, I clutched the wheel until my knuckles were white and my fingers numb. As for Lee, he sat rigidly in the passenger seat, staring straight ahead. I longed to stop the car, gather him into my arms as I had when he was a child, and tell him that everything was going to be all right. Instead, I drove on. His body posture told me, without words, that he needed to be left alone; he would deal with this in his own way. Empty words would only insult him.

Sensing his need for one more happy memory to draw from during the hard days ahead, Kay and I didn't object when the

following day Lee asked to take the boat for a final summer out-
ing with his friends before he left for the hospital. He came home
tired, but in good spirits. I doubt if any of his friends had a clue
as to how very ill he was that afternoon. They were accustomed
to his cough and his periodic hospital visits to get "cleaned out."
If they wondered why he drove the boat rather than skied, they
didn't ask.

Kay and Lee left for Salt Lake the next afternoon. We had discussed it the day before and decided the sensible thing was for
Kay to drive Lee down and stay with him while I remained at
home and worked at the office. That night, unable to shake my
fears, I could have cared less about "sensible." I was Lee's mother,
and I needed to be with him.

As promised, Kay called the next night. The central line was
in, and Lee was receiving antibiotics intravenously every six
hours. He would begin the enteral feedings later that night.
Apparently, not all patients succeeded in swallowing the "nose
hose," as the tubing was dubbed by the C/F kids; but Lee was
determined to master it, and I had no doubt that he would. The
oxygen was giving him a much-needed boost, and he was receiving drainages every few hours.

Three of his C/F friends were also in the hospital; one was his
roommate and the others were just down the hall. They dropped
by Lee's room often to compare notes and chat. I still had a hard
time with that. I realized that their camaraderie made the long
hospital stays bearable, but I worried about them trading bugs.

Ten days later, we brought Lee home. While waiting for his
discharge papers, I became acquainted with his roommate. Jim
was a young man from Montana who looked to be about twenty
years old, and he looked terrible. His body was so emaciated that
his joints appeared too large for his limbs. His lips and nails were
blue from severe hypoxemia, and he was too weak to walk more
than the few feet to the bathroom. Nevertheless, his spirits were
high and his practical jokes legendary. One joke, relished and
told repeatedly by medical staff and patients alike, was played on

an unsuspecting nurse who was new to the floor. After drawing blood from the catheter in Jim's arm, she flushed the lock with heparin. Jim waited until she had shot in the last of the heparin; then, with a horrible gurgling sound, he clawed at his throat and gasped, "That wasn't heparin, was it? I'm allergic to heparin." Sprawling backward onto his pillow, he twitched a few times, relaxed his hold on his throat, and lay limp as death. The horrified nurse screamed and hit the emergency button. His roommate, also taken in by the convincing performance, leaped out of bed and ran for help. The nurse, I'm told, never wholly forgave Jim; but to the patients on the fifth floor, he was a living legend. He and Lee became fast friends.

I was shocked when I saw all the paraphernalia we were to take home. Surveying the pumps, syringes, tubes, vials of antibiotics, and cases of the nutrient Pulmocare, I hoped Lee was, as he assured me, a "pro" at using all of it!

Fortunately, he was. Even so, getting ready for the night proved to be quite an undertaking. First came the enteral feeding. He filled the "feeding" bag with Pulmocare and hooked it on the arm of his I.V. stand, then smeared lubricating jelly on the end of the tube dangling from the bottom. "Nothing to swallowing the nose hose, once you get the hang of it," he said, tilting his head back and inserting the tube into one of his nostrils. I handed him a glass of water, and while gulping it, he slowly fed the tube down his throat. Just watching him made me gag, and I turned my head away, hoping he wouldn't notice.

When I asked him how he knew the tube was in his stomach rather than in his lungs, he shrugged. I didn't know if that meant he didn't know or if he knew and couldn't explain. I could only hope he knew, because getting liquid into a lung would be disastrous.

Tube down, he opened the clips on the tubing, programmed a small pump attached to his I.V. stand, and flipped on the switch. Slowly the formula, which looked like melted ice cream, flowed down the tube, wound around some sort of gadget on the pump that regulated its flow, and finally disappeared into Lee's nose on the last leg of its journey into his stomach.

Now it was time to move on to the antibiotics. Disinfecting and accessing the central line with one hand was awkward for him, so I took care of that while he programmed still another pump which automatically delivered an exact amount of medication per second into his vein. What a wonderfully convenient way to administer meds, especially when compared to the old method in which I was continually having to adjust the I.V. flow!

I'd had his oxygen concentrator checked and disinfected while he was in Salt Lake, so all we had to do was flip on the switch. Propped up against his pillows, Lee surveyed the many tubes connecting him to his equipment and commented ruefully, "Now, if I don't move wrong and hang myself, I should be all set."

Exhausted, he fell asleep. An hour later the pump gave a warning beep; he opened his eyes long enough to assure himself that I was disengaging the I.V. and then fell asleep again. He had set his alarm for 3:00 a.m. It would then be time to take the handful of enzymes next to a glass of water on the nightstand. Just as he had to take enzymes before his regular meals, he had to take them during the night to digest his enteral feeding. Seconds before the alarm rang, I uncurled from my chair and reached over and turned it off. I touched Lee's shoulder and handed him the pills and water. He downed them in one gulp; and, too sleepy to ask why I was still there, he settled back down.

In the dim glow of the nightlight, I gazed around my son's room. On one side of his bed, the concentrator hissed out its life-sustaining oxygen. On the other side, equipment and tubes hung from the arms of an I.V. pole like ribbons from a grotesque maypole. His tilt table, with its nebulizing equipment and compressor, was shoved against one wall; and on the stand by his bed, the luminous glow of his clock revealed a battery of pill bottles, alcohol swabs, and syringes. The place looked more like a hospital room than a young man's bedroom. Still, if it bought us some time . . .

In two hours, it would be 5:00 a.m. and time for me to begin his inhalation treatment. That finished, I would need to connect his I.V. so it could run while I got ready for work. The smart thing would be to go to bed and catch a couple hours of sleep. But I didn't want to be smart. I wanted to sit by my son.

If Lee battled personal demons, he did it without comment. On the surface, at least, he was as cheerful and independent as always. Watching him take off with friends to a movie or party, I thought how shocked they would be if they were to see him during the night. Except for the meds, they had no idea what he was doing to survive. They were only acquainted with those because rather than go home when it was time for his I.V., he would go into the bathroom, access the central line, and return to the party, pump in hand.

Exactly one week after Lee arrived home from the University of Utah Medical Center, we were racing back to the C/F Center. The afternoon before, he had complained of shortness of breath and said that his chest felt like it was being squeezed in a vise. By evening, he was running a fever.

The night seemed a hundred years long. I wanted to take him to the emergency room at St. Luke's, but he was adamant that we wait and call Dr. Kane in Salt Lake in the morning. Since I couldn't physically toss him in the car, he won. To make matters worse, Kay had left that morning for a World War II marine pilot reunion in Cherry Point, North Carolina.

It was nearly noon before Lee finally reached his doctor. Hanging up the phone, he said in a strained voice, "Dr. Kane thinks it's a pneumothorax, and he wants us at the University Medical Center before six o'clock. We'll have to hurry."

"What about hospitalizing you here?" I cried. "If you have a hole in your lung, I'd think he'd want you admitted into the nearest hospital! And what about oxygen on the way? We haven't any portable tanks."

"He said he wants me down there. He didn't say anything about oxygen, and we don't have time to get tanks and be there before six. I'll be okay without. Let's get going."

Thirty minutes later, we had our bags and Lee's equipment piled into the car and were on the freeway headed for Salt Lake. In Twin Falls we stopped and picked up my sister, Elva. In case Lee ran into trouble enroute, I wanted someone with me. I'd phoned her before we left, and she was standing at the door, bag in hand, when we drove up.

Lee was in serious trouble by the time we crossed the state line into Utah, and we still had over a hundred miles to go. We'd made good time crossing the desert, but now we were entering the Wasatch Front where traffic was heavy, especially this time of day. I thought of the little girl who only a few years before had died in her parents' car as they had made a similar run for this same hospital. I floored the accelerator, and with Elva as lookout, I cut crazily in and out of the crowded lanes of traffic.

"Driving like a maniac is going to get you a ticket or get us killed. Either way, we'll lose time!" Lee complained from the back seat.

"I'd gladly pay a ticket for a police escort," I responded. "You just hang in there, and don't worry about my driving."

At the hospital, Dr. Kane immediately clamped an oxygen mask on Lee's face and ordered an x-ray. The nurse suggested that Elva and I go to the cafeteria and get something to eat. They wouldn't know anything until after they had the x-ray results.

Elva and I grabbed a sandwich and returned to Lee's room to find it overflowing with medical personnel. A doctor was lowering Lee into a wheel chair while an intern, swearing softly, tried to attach a portable oxygen tank to it. "There's no time for that," the doctor snapped. "We have to get him downstairs."

Lee sank into the wheelchair, his face a ghastly blue-gray. I shoved my way toward him, Elva close behind. Someone dumped a load of equipment into my arms and with a short, "Follow me," grabbed the wheelchair and ran toward the elevator. Elva, too, received her share to carry, and together we raced down the hall behind the flying chair and its passenger. The elevator doors closed behind us, and the doctor said hurriedly, "I don't have time to explain now. The x-ray showed a large, left pneumothorax with a mediastinal shift, and when that happens, there's no time to lose."

The elevator doors opened, and quickly he shoved the wheelchair through. We raced down another hall, ending up in a small room where he relieved us of our burdens, motioned us toward a bench, and disappeared with Lee through some partitioning drapes. Terrified, I clutched my sister's hand. A murmur of voices drifted from the cubicle. We strained to hear, but caught only enough to know they were going to insert a tube in Lee's chest.

The tube in place, Lee was brought back to the same bed he had vacated only a week before. Dr. Kane stayed late into the evening, puzzled by Lee's fever. He said that normally a pneumothorax doesn't cause a fever; and, with all the antibiotics pouring into him, it was unlikely that he had an infection.

I had intended to stay all night with Lee, but he whispered that he'd rather I'd leave and come back in the morning. Elva and I spent the night with her son, Scott, who lived near the hospital.

Dr. Kane and Dr. Black were already in Lee's room when I arrived early the next morning. Lee had had a bad night. His bed was piled high with extra blankets, but still he shook with chills. His temperature was 104 degrees, and even with the oxygen he struggled to breathe. Dr. Kane decided that he must be having a reaction to piperacillin, the antibiotic he had been taking intravenously for several weeks, and ordered it stopped immediately.

In the meantime, Lee's latest x-ray showed an increase in the size of the pneumothorax. Dr. Kane ordered a suction bottle, and supply sent one up that was new to the doctors. For the next thirty minutes, they tried to determine how it worked. Watching, I felt as if I'd wandered into the middle of a TV situation comedy. The more frustrated they became, the more determined they were to make it work. At one point, one doctor lay prone on the floor while the other sat cross-legged beside him, reading instructions. All the while, nurses and resident doctors stepped over and around them as if this were an everyday occurrence. I wondered if this challenge was a welcome diversion from their daily life-and-death decisions or if they were, in truth, a pair of frustrated would-be mechanics. In the end, someone else wandered in—another doctor, a patient's mechanically minded father, who knows? At any rate, he made a suggestion, and the equipment started doing its thing. I half expected "high fives" all around, but self-congratulatory grins sufficed.

Lee's reaction to the piperacillin had not only made his white count practically nil, but had also stopped the production of red blood cells in his bone marrow, so Dr. Kane ordered blood transfusions. The lung didn't heal, and two days later the doctor injected quinacrine, an irritating solution, into the tube in Lee's chest in the hope that it would sear the surface of the lung and cause it to adhere to the lung surface inside the chest cavity. In spite of receiving a shot of demerol to dull the pain, Lee turned deathly pale and knotted the sheet in his clenched fists.

In order to expose as much of the pleural surface as possible to the quinacrine, Dr. Kane had me change Lee's position every fifteen minutes. He did well in the upright and prone positions, but when I lowered his head, he had great difficulty breathing. Nervous, I rang for the nurse. She assured me he was fine; but still, I was relieved when it was over.

The next morning, Lee experienced severe chest pains. There was a quick call to radiology, and they rolled in a portable x-ray unit. Their pictures showed that the pneumothorax was larger; and after a hurried consultation, a doctor stepped to Lee's side and said, "The tube in your chest isn't doing the job. We're going to insert a larger one beside it." Patting Lee's shoulder, he added, "You don't look like you're in the mood for a wild gurney ride, so the cardiothoracic surgeon is coming to your room. You won't even have to move out of your bed. How's that for service?"

Lee acknowledged the attempt at humor with a weak smile and nod of the head. The surgeon arrived, and Dr. Harper Randall, a favorite resident of Lee's, ushered me into a small anteroom across the hall where I could be alone to wait and pray.

Re-entering Lee's room, I was startled to see that he was connected to monitors. Reaching around the conglomeration of tubes and wires, I bent over and whispered his name. He opened pain-filled eyes, met my gaze briefly, and closed them again. His long black lashes accentuated his white face and sunken cheeks.

For the next hour, Renee, his nurse, didn't leave his side. Occasionally, his respiration dipped too low and set off an alarm. Startled, Lee would open his eyes, and Renee would quickly increase his oxygen. I sat on the other side of the bed, holding his hand, assuring him that he was going to be fine, and praying that I spoke the truth. As soon as he stabilized, they rolled his bed and equipment down the hall to a private room across from the nurses' station where they could observe him more easily. A "No Visitors" sign hung on the door.

When it became evident that Lee was in for a long hospitalization, Elva returned to Twin Falls. However, Pat, Stan, Steve, and their spouses came to the hospital often to see their brother. Although they weren't allowed in his room, they found comfort in peeking at him through the open door. Sometimes Lee would open his eyes and waggle his fingers. Then they would hug me and assure me he was going to be okay.

Lee was too ill to eat and too nauseated to tolerate the enteral feedings. He was losing weight rapidly, and Dr. Kane started an I.V. of 10% intralipids.

Kay hadn't thought to call me when he changed hotels shortly after his arrival at Cherry Point, and it took me a few days to reach him. When he finally received my message, he flew to Boise and then drove to Salt Lake City. Words can't describe the relief I felt when he walked through the door into Lee's room!

Lee was noticeably weaker the next time Dr. Kane sclerosed his lung with quinacrine. After the first sclerosing, Lee was able to help me change his positions, but the second time he hadn't the strength, and two nurses had to help me.

The third sclerosing almost proved fatal. Within seconds of Dr. Kane's injecting the quinacrine, Lee's body stiffened and his back arched. One arm flailed helplessly above his head, and the cords in his neck knotted in an effort to breath. The tracings on the monitor plummeted, and the alarms went crazy. Dr. Kane barked, "Is it the pain, Lee? Tell me, is it the pain?"

Lee managed to gasp, "Nothing to breathe with!"

I sprang from my chair to go to my dying son. Instantly, a nurse grabbed my arm and restrained me. Dr. Kane's voice cut into my consciousness. "You're okay, Lee. I'm unclamping the tube and draining it out. You'll be all right in a minute." When he recovered enough to speak, Lee said he'd felt as if his lungs were paralyzed.

Kay was away from the hospital at the time, and when he came back a few hours later he took one look at Lee's face and hurriedly left the room. I followed him to the little anteroom across the hall. He was leaning heavily against the wall, sobs wracking his body. "He's dying, isn't he?" he cried. Going to him, I put my arms around this man who had always been my rock and my strength, and this time I was the comforter.

By now, Lee had been in the hospital for eight days, and his lung continued to leak. When he was first admitted to the hospital, Dr. Kane had called in Dr. Shreekanth V. Karwande, a renowned thoracic and heart surgeon, and he had checked on Lee every day. Now the two doctors held a hurried consultation. Lee was losing ground hourly, and they felt they had no choice but to operate immediately. Sitting beside Lee's bed, Dr. Karwande quickly made a sketch of his lungs and showed us what he intended to do. When he finished, Lee whispered that he'd like a few minutes alone before they took him to the operating room. We left the room. When we went back in, Lee's face was pale, but he was composed and told us he was ready. I held his hand until we reached the surgical area. There, I gave him a quick kiss and watched them wheel him through the door and out of sight.

I didn't realize I was crying until Kay reached over and wiped away my tears. All I knew was that, in spite of telling myself that Lee was going to live, I was suffocating with fear. Out of the corner of my eye, I saw Kay pop a nitro pill under his tongue and wondered how many he had taken during the preceding hours.

Kay and I rejoined our children and their spouses; together we waited, silently praying for Lee and for his surgeon. Finally it was over, and the pleased look on Dr. Karwande's face as he strode down the hall told us that the operation had been a success. There had been ten blebs (bubbles or blisters) on the lung surface in Lee's lung. He had stapled them closed and peeled the lining off the top half of the lung. The lung should now glue itself to the chest wall and not collapse again. The challenge would be to prevent his lungs from filling with mucus. A therapist would clap his chest every few hours during the night; and, as excruciating as it would be, Lee must cough hard enough to rid his airways of the clogging mucus.

I had seen Kay immediately following his two major surgeries, so I was better prepared than he was to see Lee. Even so, the intensive care room tilted crazily. Except for the rising and falling of his chest as the respirator breathed for him, he appeared lifeless. Reaching through the profusion of tubes, I found his hand and squeezed it. There was no response. The Lee part of him wasn't there. I could only pray that it would return.

A few days later, Lee had a surprise visit from his friend, Scott Wolfley. At first, Lee's nurse in SICU said he couldn't go in, but when we told her how far Scott had come and that he could take our turn (our visits were limited to a few minutes an hour), she consented.

When he heard Scott was there, Lee asked the nurse to help him into the chair by his bed. He didn't want to appear sick in front of his friend! Scott was allowed to stay fifteen minutes, and then the nurse shooed him out and helped Lee back into his bed. Reassured that his pal was going to make it, Scott headed back to Boise. By the time he arrived home, he had spent nearly twelve hours on the road for a few minutes' visit with his friend. Later, he told us it was well worth it. As for Lee, wiped out and hurting, he fell asleep as soon as Scott left, a pleased smile on his lips.

Five days after the operation, Lee was moved out of intensive care, and I returned home to go back to work. Kay stayed with Lee.

Lee had been home from the hospital only a few days when Scott invited him to lunch at a rather crowded restaurant. I thought this might create a problem because Dr. Karwande had warned him not to get his rib cage bumped. However, Lee solved the problem by using his grandfather's cane. He explained, "I don't need it for support. It's just a deterrent from being jostled in the crowd. No one bumps someone walking with a cane." The kid almost kills himself to portray the virile American male, and then he voluntarily carries a cane? As if reading my mind, he grinned and said, "Canes and crutches are okay, because everyone assumes you're an athlete recovering from an injury."

I looked at his hundred-pound body, with its gaunt face and sunken eyes, and shook my head. By no stretch of the imagination did he look like a wounded athlete! A husband and four sons notwithstanding, I would never understand male logic!

This was definitely not Lee's year. Exactly three weeks to the day he was discharged from the Utah Medical Center, he was back in the hospital—this time in St. Luke's in Boise. The pneumonia struck in the night, and by the time we reached the hospital he was suffering a severe deficiency of oxygen. That night, both Lee's and my spirits hit an all-time low. After a couple of hours of desultory conversation, he said, "Why don't you go on home? There's nothing you can do here, and I need some sleep." Halfway home, I couldn't see the road for tears and pulled into a parking lot. I wondered if Lee was crying, too.

As his strength returned, so did his desire to get on with his life. In the middle of December he left for the Salt Lake area, ostensibly to visit family and friends, but I suspected it was to scout out job opportunities—this, in spite of his doctors' admonitions that he must not even consider taking on full-time employment. He returned a few days later. He didn't mention having had any job interviews, and I didn't inquire. Dreams were to die hard in this youngest son of mine; but even as I grieved at the pain they caused him, I wondered if it was those very dreams that were keeping him alive.

—1988—

Lee was hospitalized at the University of Utah Medical Center in March, and when he faced hospitalization again in April, he decided to move to Salt Lake. "I need to stop bouncing my health care back and forth between Boise and Salt Lake," he explained. "Now that I'm sick more often, Salt Lake with its C/F Clinic seems the logical choice."

With a heavy heart, I watched Kay and Roger load the pickup with a spare bed, a chest of drawers, the portable tilt table, and odds and ends of furniture. Lee would store it at Steve's until he was out of the hospital and had found an apartment.

The plan was for Kay and me to drive the pickup to Salt Lake and for Lee to drive his car. However, as I stepped into the truck, I looked back and saw him leaning against the side of his car. Walking the few yards from the house to the driveway had exhausted him. I walked back and slid into the driver's seat. Without comment, he handed me the keys. How could he ever live alone in Salt Lake?

The last day we were at the Medical Center before returning home, Lee was in high spirits. Pat and Robert had offered him a job keeping the Quick Stop books; and Eric, an inhalation therapist with a five-year-old daughter, had invited him to share an apartment with them. Eric had wanted to move into a nicer apartment for some time, but needed someone to share expenses. "Just think," Lee said happily, "the next time you come down, I'll have my own pad!"

I forced myself to smile and tell him how wonderful that was going to be, then I kissed him goodbye. At the door, I looked back. He lifted his hand to wave but went into a convulsive coughing spell that knotted the cords in his neck and turned his face blue. I rushed to his side and pounded his back until he coughed up the choking mucus. We said goodbye again; then I turned and walked blindly from the room.

On a Friday in August, I came home from work to find Kay in the back yard barbecuing hamburgers for Lee and one of his C/F friends, Charlie Stockdale. Karen Hirsch, a nurse from the Medical Center's fifth floor where they house the C/F patients, had driven them to Boise to attend the wedding of one of their nurses. The next afternoon the doorbell rang, and we had another surprise. There stood DeeAnn Gerold, also a nurse from fifth floor. She, too, had driven from Salt Lake to attend Patty's wedding, and with her was James Bridenbaker, another of Lee's C/F friends. He had been too ill to travel when Karen had left the day before, but here he was, one day later, out on a hospital pass and on our doorstep!

DeeAnn needed help getting him out of her car, and Lee and Kay rushed out to assist her. With Kay managing the oxygen cart and Lee and DeeAnn supporting him, James made his way into the house. Exhausted, he collapsed on the couch to rest before attempting the few steps down to Lee's room. Once down the stairs, he gratefully sank onto the bed. Lee slipped his shoes off and covered him with an afghan. Breathing heavily, his face gray and lips and nails blue, James nevertheless managed to grin and whisper "Thank you" before exhaustion closed his eyes. DeeAnn took his pulse; and then, patting his thin shoulder, she turned, indicating we should leave and let him rest.

Back upstairs, I whispered, "He's so ill; perhaps we should ask Lee's doctor to contact Dr. Kane in Salt Lake and get him admitted into the hospital here."

DeeAnn shook her head. "He'll be okay. He's just worn out from the ride. I'll let him sleep for an hour and then give him a treatment. Tomorrow morning I'll pick him up and take him back to the hospital."

"You're leaving him with us overnight?" I exclaimed, too alarmed to be tactful.

"That's all right, isn't it?" she asked, surprised. "Just before we left, we discovered that the people where we'd arranged to stay smoke. So, of course, he can't stay with them."

The thought of being responsible for such a dangerously ill young man panicked me. "We'd love to have both of you stay with us," I offered. "We have plenty of room, and I'm sure you'd feel more at ease about James if you were close by." I managed not to add that I would certainly feel more at ease with her nearby. However, she said that James would be fine; and, after giving him a treatment, off she went to her friend's home to get ready for the wedding, confident that all would be well. I watched her drive away, hoping that her confidence was born of professional wisdom rather than the optimism of youth!

I didn't see how James could possibly attend the wedding, especially when Lee was too short of breath to be of much assistance. But once again, I underestimated these kids' willpower. When it was time to go, James rallied; Lee helped him get ready, and off they went. I stood at the window, watching them drive away. James waved and flashed his famous grin. What an easy boy to love!

After they left, I moved Lee's oxygen concentrator into the family room and made up a bed on the couch. James would be sleeping in Lee's room, and I knew Lee would want to be near in case he had trouble. Lee had told me before he left that the wedding was a formal Catholic one with mass, followed by a reception and dance. "We probably won't be home until around two," he said. "You go to bed; I can get James into the house alone."

"I'm sure you can," I agreed, "but it'll be easier if I give you a hand."

I was surprised when they returned shortly after eleven o'clock. I helped Lee get James into his room, and then Lee took over. Through the closed door, I could hear James' strangling cough, and then the sound of clapping. Lee was giving his friend a drainage. When I asked if I could help, Lee said everything was under control. But, if I wanted, I could bring in another oxygen tank from the car. James was going through it fast. Also, he wouldn't mind if I gave him a short treatment when he finished with James. He was a little short of breath himself, and maybe that would move the stuff around.

While I gave Lee his treatment, he told me about the wedding. He had had a good time, but James had almost passed out a couple of times, and he thought he'd better get him home. "Actually, I was ready myself," he acknowledged. "I've been coughing more this past week. Sure hope it's only a plug, because I've planned on doing some serious water skiing at our family reunion next weekend."

The remainder of the night lasted just short of forever. I was anxious about James and tiptoed down the stairs every few minutes, peeking through the crack in his door to make certain he was all right. Often, Lee was already there, adjusting his oxygen, clapping his back, or giving him medication. Hearing the gentleness in his voice brought a lump to my throat. This was the tender, caring side of Lee that few people saw.

The next morning, Lee and I had a hurried consultation. James had finally fallen into a peaceful sleep, and we disliked waking him. Yet, in an hour we'd need to leave for Irene's ward sacrament meeting, where our newest grandson would be blessed. If James needed a treatment, we would have to get it started. We might as well have let him sleep, because when Lee woke him, he said he was too tired for a drainage and would sleep until DeeAnn came to pick him up. She could give him one then. Reluctantly, we left him in bed and took off for the church. By the time we came home, the bed was empty and James was on his way back to the Salt Lake hospital.

Helping Lee move the concentrator back into his room, I commented, "I don't think it was very smart of James' doctor to give him permission to make such a long trip when he was so ill."

Lee shrugged. "James is to the point where nothing much is going to affect the outcome. I guess the doctors think he may as well enjoy the little time he has left." However, the concern in his eyes belied the casualness of his words, and that night I overheard him talking to James on the phone, making certain that he had arrived safely at the hospital.

Lee became close friends with several nurses and resident doctors during his frequent hospital stays, and they often included him in their activities. He especially loved those that involved the outdoors. In September he wrote, "I'm back from the canoe trip I mentioned in my letter last week. The fires in Yellowstone Park made going there impossible, so we went instead to Jackson Lake in the Grand Teton National Park. Six of us went: Beth Evans and Karen Hirsch, both fifth floor C/F nurses; Cindy, a pediatric nurse; Andy Reilly, formerly from England and now a professor at the University of Utah, and Ray Blatoe, a 6'6" Air Force engineer who works on fighter jets.

"This was my first trip, and I was quite concerned that I might hold the others back; but I found canoeing to be quite easy. It only required upper body strength, and I never really got winded. The only time I had problems was when we portaged about a quarter of a mile in one area. Andy and Ray carried the heavy stuff, leaving only light things for me to carry. They didn't seem to mind.

"It was quite fun going with these people because they understood my limitations and were willing to give me treatments. There was no electricity to run my nebulizer, but I took a couple shots from an inhalator, and then Beth gave me chest physiotherapy just like she does in the hospital.

"It helped that the group didn't want to do things in packs. If I fell behind, it was no problem; they just rested or fished while they waited for me.

"I wish you could have been with us to see the beautiful scenery. I can't describe it, but I hope you can get the general idea from the pictures I'm sending. The fire gave everything an added dimension. During the day the haze gave the mountains an ethereal look; and at night it turned the moon a blood red. It was sobering to lie in our sleeping bags and watch the flames light up the sky. It was so peaceful where we were that it was difficult to comprehend the destruction the fire was causing in the Park.

"I'm sure Mom is wondering how I did physically. Well, I lost some weight in spite of the good food we ate—steak, potatoes, chicken, chili, Andy's famous spaghetti, and lots of granola, anything to keep energy up. I guess it was not having the enteral feedings or nighttime oxygen. But I did well, and I'm glad they invited me to go along. I hope I get to go on more trips and explore more of this part of the country."

Monday, September 26, 1988—Excerpts from Lee's tape:

"This tape is about my trip to the Canyonlands National Park in Utah. Beth Evans, Andy Reilly, Charlie Stockdale, a guy named Patric from France, and I took the five-day trip, four days on the bikes and one day getting there and back.

"This being my first mountain bike trip, I didn't realize how hard mountain biking can be. It's a lot different than biking around the city on paved roads! There are washboards, sand, and rocks, all sorts of things to contend with. You have to really concentrate because such a simple thing as hitting your pedal on a rock can make your bike skip out from under you, or you may go flying over the handlebars if you catch your front wheel in a rut. Maybe that's why it's a lot more fun than regular bike riding!

"Biking down the sides of the cliffs was really something. The trails were narrow with deep ruts and covered with large, loose rocks, and so steep that our bikes literally flew. The trail was one switchback right after the other. Just before hitting one, we'd slam on our brakes to make the 180-degree turn, come out of it, release our brakes, and go flying again to the next one. I've never experienced anything so exhilarating before. My bike vibrated and bounced, wind whipped through my hair, and my heart raced as I used all my strength to negotiate the turns, narrowly missing rocks and unexpected ruts that threatened to upend me. Totally alive and in command, there were only my bike and me careening down that canyon wall! It was like C/F and hospitals didn't exist.

"Everyone took a turn driving the 4-Runner; but since Charlie and I were the only ones with C/F and weren't in great shape to begin with, we drove it more than the others, especially toward the end when we started wearing down.

"All in all, it was a great trip. The pictures I have will give you more of an idea and insight as to what the trails look like."

On October 4, Lee called me from the hospital and in a matter-of-fact tone told me that he had cepacia. Pseudomonas cepacia is a virulent bacterium which is almost totally resistant to antibiotics, and most C/F patients deteriorate quickly once it colonizes in their lungs. "I was really low right after the doctor told me," he said. "I figured that after all my near misses, this time it was for real, and there was nothing I could do about it. But I'm okay now. Probably what helped me the most was remembering Dr. Venning saying that every time he thought there was nothing more he could do for me, along came a new antibiotic and we'd be off and running again. That's bound to happen again this time.

"Then, too," he continued, "one of my friends dropped by. He said he's had cepacia for over two years and is getting along quite well. He told me a few of the other older kids have it, too, and they're still around. From what I hear, some only last a few months after it shows up, and others get along fairly well for a couple of years or so. Maybe there are different kinds of strains, I don't know. No one around here seems to know much about it. If I find out anything new, I'll let you know."

Shocked, I asked shakily, "What are they doing for you?"

"They have me on tobramycin and an antibiotic I haven't had before. It's called aztreonam. I don't know if it's for the cepacia or not. From what the doctor told me, my sputum cultures show that my type of cepacia is resistant to all antibiotics. But I'm feeling better, and may even get a pass from the hospital tomorrow to take James for a short ride in the canyon. The leaves are starting to change color, and the canyon is beautiful this time of year."

"That will be nice," I answered, my mind still reeling from

what he had told me. "Back to cepacia. Did the doctor say how you contracted it? Is it transmissible?"

"No. Anyway, all the doctors I've talked to here say it isn't. It just seems to be another strain of pseudomonas that some C/F kids get. And, Mom, I don't want you worrying yourself silly about this. Except for that dumb promise I made that I wouldn't hold anything back, I wouldn't have said anything. There's no sense worrying about something you can't do anything about."

I told him we'd leave at noon and be in Salt Lake by evening. He said he'd rather we'd wait and come later.

Kay and I often cried for Lee, but rarely in front of each other. That morning, however, we clung together and wept. Then, cried out, we straightened up, blew our noses, and Kay went into the backyard to finish picking the grapes while I bottled the juice. Our hands were busy at home, but our hearts were in a hospital room in Salt Lake City.

Two weeks later, Lee called to tell us that he had been discharged from the hospital. His doctor had told him that for now, at least, the cepacia was under control. Why, he didn't know, since it was supposed to be antibiotic-resistant.

Just before hanging up, he added almost as an afterthought, "Oh, yeah, it's no biggie, but I'd better let you know. I'm on insulin shots for the diabetes now. No big deal, just one more thing I do to take care of the old bod. Also, I'm not assimilating enough vitamins from my food, so they've started me on megadoses of Vitamin A to protect my sight. While they were at it, the doctor tested my hearing and more or less confirmed what we already knew. He said my hearing loss is mostly in the mid-frequencies, with the right ear worse than the left. I asked him if it was caused by the antibiotics, and he said that loss of hearing can be a side effect of one of the drugs I'm taking, but that mine was more typical of a hereditary pattern than of being drug induced. Of course, it doesn't really matter," he added indifferently. "Even if the antibiotic is doing it, I still have to keep taking it, don't I?"

Heartsick, I acknowledged that that was true. Our son was

dying by inches, and we were helpless to stop it.

A week later, he moved from the apartment he shared with the therapist and his daughter into a small furnished apartment closer to the hospital. He would be living alone, but he wasn't concerned about being lonely. He would be getting some temporary work again soon; and there was always someone from the hospital, either staff member or patient, available for socializing. In fact, he was planning a mountain biking trip to the Slick Rock Festival in Moab, Utah, with his friends on Halloween.

One week he was in the hospital, and the next week he was planning a mountain biking trip! Was everyone crazy?

In late November, the family congregated in Pat and Robert's home in Orem for Thanksgiving dinner. Lee looked white and frail, having been released from the hospital less than a week before. At first he acted withdrawn, almost like a soldier on furlough from a war that was impossible for him to share even with those he loved. However, as the afternoon wore on he acted more like himself, and even succumbed to the pleading of his nieces and nephews for a story about his adventures in the "wilderness."

"It was the second night of our Canyonlands biking trip," he began in his best storytelling voice, "and we had this big pot of chili for dinner. Now, usually we secured all the leftover food in the 4-Runner because the mice that live in the desert aren't like any mice you've ever seen. They're little, but they have big, sharp teeth that can chew through any box you leave out, no matter how strong." He paused for effect, and the little girls shuddered deliciously at the thought of mice with giant, sharp teeth while the little boys stoutly maintained that they'd kill any old mouse that chewed on their boxes.

"Like I said," he continued, "we had this big pot of chili for dinner; and, even though we stuffed ourselves, we couldn't quite eat it all. We decided to save it for breakfast, and because it was in a cast iron pot with a lid, we didn't put it in the 4-Runner. After all, little mice can't lift a heavy lid, can they?" The children agreed that only Super Mouse could do that, and these were just plain, ordinary desert mice.

"Well, the next morning when Patric took off the lid, what did he see but eight little red-stained feet sticking up out of the chili! Two little mice had managed to squirm under the lid and jump into the chili during the night, and had drowned."

"What did you do then?" one of the nieces asked anxiously.

"We were hungry, so we fished them out by their little feet and ate them along with the rest of the chili," he told her, smacking his lips. The little girl promptly gagged, and Lee quickly dumped her off his lap, confessing, "Hey, I was just teasing. Actually, after all of us had taken a peek at the strange sight, Andy took the chili and the mice and gave them a proper burial in the sand."

"You have lots of fun, don't you, Uncle Lee?" one of his little nephews said enviously.

Lee roughed up his hair and replied, "Yes, life is good. Enjoy it."

In the summer of 1989, Lee was accepted for an accounting internship in Betheseda, Maryland. This photo was taken at the fountain in front of the White House.

—1989—

Frank, a C/F young adult we'd met at the Salt Lake Clinic, passed away in January. Shortly after returning from his funeral, Lee called.

"I roomed with Frank a few times in the hospital," he related, "but I didn't know him well. His big dream was to be a drummer in a heavy metal band; and when he wanted to make a statement, he dressed the part, wearing sleeveless shirts with heavy metal logos, pants with gaping holes, an earring, and the whole bit. Deep down, though, he was a tender guy.

"I'll never forget one stunt he pulled when we roomed together. James and Charlie were visiting me, and I don't know if he was bored by our chit-chat or what, but without warning he leaped on the wide windowsill, dropped his pants, and mooned out of the window. Being five stories up, of course, no one saw him. Frustrated by the lack of attention, he pried the window open a few inches and screamed at the top of his lungs, 'Hey, look up here, look up here!'

"Unfortunately, his shouts attracted the wrong audience. Those down below, oblivious to the antics far above their heads, didn't break stride. But his cries sent all the fifth floor medical personnel within earshot into action.

"Dr. Taylor and a nurse were the first to race through the door. Skidding to a stop in the middle of the room, they stood stock still at the sight before them. There, on top of the sill, stood a startled Frank, suddenly much more exposed than he had intended, while James, Charlie, and I rolled on my bed with laughter.

"We were still chuckling about it when Frank saw the security people coming. Thinking he was in serious trouble, he took off down the back stairwell and didn't come back to the hospital for a couple of hours. Actually, the security people had only come to bolt the window closed so there wouldn't be any more mooning."

"I wish Frank had been able to realize his dream of being a drummer with a big band—at least for a little while," he said.

I remembered Lee's long-ago dream of owning a little soup and sandwich shop, and wondered if he thought about it anymore.

Monday, March 13, 1989—Letter from Lee:

"Dear Mom and Dad—A quick note to say hello. James is still in the hospital, but the doctors say he'll be ready for the trip to Huntington Beach with Charlie and me next week. Charlie and I are still cleaned out from our incarceration last month, so we're okay.

"I worked last week for Procter & Gamble. I'm glad I'm busy and keeping my mind occupied. Been thinking about things too much, as is.

"Well, I'm off for a haircut. Don't get too overjoyed, Mom. It's only a trim! Love, Lee."

March 1989—Excerpts from Lee's tape:

"This tape is about Charlie, James, and my trip to California and Tijuana.

"Charlie was going to Huntington, California and stay with his Aunt Nancy and Uncle Dave during his spring break from college, and he invited James and me to go along. James' health was deteriorating, and we didn't know if he should try to go or not. But he decided to go, and I'm glad because this may have been the last fun trip of his life, and it was a time for just the three of us to be together. The big problem was how to provide him with enough oxygen to get him to California. Portable tanks don't hold many hours, especially at the rate James goes through it. We finally solved it by borrowing Dirk McBride's liquid oxygen system called a "cow." The cow looks like a beer keg, except it's about twice the size; and oxygen can either be run directly off it or it can be used to fill up a portable unit to carry around. It weighs probably fifty or sixty pounds, but has rollers on the bottom which makes it manageable.

"We buckled the cow to the back seat of Charlie's Toyota, and James breathed off it while he was in the car. He used his portable units when he walked around and explored with us. It worked out very nicely.

"Because I was going water skiing at Lake Powell right after the trip, I drove my truck to Richfield, and Charlie and James picked me up there. It took us about sixteen hours to get to Huntington. Charlie and I were apprehensive about letting James drive in the California traffic because he has a reputation of being rather casual at the wheel; but when he insisted that it was his turn, we said okay and fastened our seat belts. Actually, he did very well.

"We made our headquarters with Dave and Nancy and fanned out from there on little side trips to various beaches and scenic areas. At first we limited ourselves, because we didn't want James to get too tired. However, he was holding up well and eager for excitement, so we decided to go to Tijuana.

"We parked the car on the United States side of customs and walked across the border. Tijuana proved to be a fascinating place, and we went exploring before returning to the shopping area where I bought a couple of blankets, and the three of us bought matching Tijuana T-shirts.

"James is extremely oxygen dependent and, although the dial on his portable tank showed more than enough oxygen to get him back to Huntington, we didn't want to take any chances, so we started back toward customs. When we were about two hundred yards from customs, the unthinkable happened. James' oxygen ran out! Later, we learned that the tank had a defective dial. To say we were scared witless was not the half of it. We knew we had to get him out of Tijuana and back to the States where we could get help. Luckily, we were at sea level, which gave him an edge. It took us at least an hour to make that two hundred yards to customs. He'd walk a few feet and rest, then another few feet and rest. Even so, he was tight and straining.

"When things go wrong, they really go wrong! When we came out of customs, we were in a different area from where we went in, and we weren't sure where the parking lot was. Charlie went to look for the car while I stayed with James.

"About half an hour later, Charlie was back. We loaded up our stuff, helped James into the back seat, and told him to lie down and keep calm. He was tight and anxious. His nails were quite blue, but his lips weren't too bad. We felt he would be okay as long as he conserved his energy and didn't try to talk.

"After about an hour on the road, James got into real trouble and told us we had to get him to a hospital fast. At the first hospital sign we pulled off, but there were no more signs directing us. We pulled into a small fruit stand and asked the owner where the hospital was. He didn't know, so we called the hospital to get directions. More problems! We were new to the area and couldn't understand the directions. Luckily, a lady at the stand saw James struggling to breathe and got on the line and clarified the directions for us.

"At the hospital, two nurses helped James into a wheelchair and wheeled him into the emergency room, telling Charlie and me to wait. Two hours later, we were still waiting and getting really anxious. We finally got the girl at the desk to go and see what was happening. When she came back she told us that James was fine, but they were having problems getting his oxygen tank refilled.

"The hospital where we'd ended up was a small for-profit hospital. They didn't have the facilities to refill James' tank, and they wouldn't loan us one of theirs, even though we promised to return it. After calling around, the secretary located a private company who would fill James' tank for $125.00 which, of course, was outrageous. He said he wouldn't do it for less because it was after hours, and he wouldn't accept an insurance card or a personal check. It had to be cash.

"In the meantime, the doctor wanted to hospitalize James. We knew that would be disastrous. Just during the few hours we'd been there, we could tell they hadn't had much experience with C/F, at least not with anyone as bad as James. He panicked at the thought of getting caught there and insisted on leaving. The hospital had him sign a release saying that if anything happened, they weren't responsible. James signed and walked out. Charlie and I trailed along behind him, wondering if we were doing the right thing.

"As we were getting in the car, the respiratory therapist came out and said to James, 'Look, come in through the back door and let me give you a treatment. That will at least dilate your bronchial tubes until you get to Huntington.' We slipped through the back door into an examining room where she met us and gave him a good treatment. We thanked her profusely and told her if she was ever in Salt Lake to give us a call.

"Charlie and I were still nervous about taking James without oxygen, but about ten minutes into the ride he fell asleep and slept all the way to Huntington Beach. Once back to the condo, he hooked himself to his oxygen, and everything was fine.

"On the way back to Salt Lake, Charlie and James dropped me off at Richfield where I picked up my truck and headed for Lake Powell. There, I hooked up with Russ Peterson and did some serious water skiing, which wore me out pretty good! James and Charlie continued on to Salt Lake, getting there at ten or eleven that night. James checked back into the hospital, tired and happy, seemingly none the worse for wear, and Charlie went back to his studies."

In April, Lee called and said he was coming home to talk, and he might not return to Salt Lake. He didn't say what was wrong, but he sounded as if he'd been crying. I'd only heard Lee cry twice since he was a little boy, and both times he'd been expressing his love for his family. For some time, however, I'd felt that something was wrong. Often when the family was together, I'd glimpse a flat look in his eyes when he thought no one was looking.

Arriving home, he talked to Kay and me long into the night. He was full of doubts about God, the truthfulness of the gospel, everything. Spiritually, he was at a crossroads. He must decide between the gospel and the inactive lifestyle he was falling into.

Although it was after midnight when we finally went to bed, my pain was too great to sleep, and at 4:00 a.m. I dressed, grabbed a flashlight, and took off into the early morning darkness where I walked the quiet residential streets until dawn. Never before had I suffered such exquisite pain or been so frightened—not even when I thought he was dying. Then it had been his mortal life at risk; now, unless he regained his testimony, it could be much more—his exaltation could be in jeopardy.

As I walked, I reviewed his life. As a child, he reveled in Bible and Book of Mormon stories, and he and his brothers often acted them out in family home evening. During his teens, the years when doubts most often arise, he had manifested unwavering faith in the Lord and in the priesthood. I recalled his desire to go on a mission, and his disappointment when his health didn't permit it. I thought of his many callings in the Church as a young adult, from Primary teacher to elders quorum secretary. I couldn't remember a time in Boise or at BYU when he hadn't had a Church calling. When had doubts begun to creep in? Had they been there before he left home, and we weren't aware of them? Or had they started after he moved away?

We knew he had never felt a part of his ward in Salt Lake City. His first apartment was in an older area of the city, and the ward was composed almost exclusively of middle-aged and elderly members who had been friends for years. No one seemed to notice the quiet boy who sat by himself for a few Sundays, then disappeared for two or three Sundays, only to appear a week or two later, as he went in and out of the hospital. He had introduced himself to his elders quorum president and the bishopric, but they were in a hurry and he didn't push it.

After several unsuccessful attempts, he did finally succeed in making an appointment with the bishop, but when he arrived at his office the bishop had forgotten and wasn't there. The executive secretary promised to make another appointment and give Lee a call. No call came, and when I urged him to take the initiative again, he replied, "I don't really care whether I meet with him now or not." The bitterness in his voice frightened me, and I reminded him that his salvation was his personal responsibility, not that of the bishop or anyone else.

In stark contrast to the ward, his C/F friends and many of the hospital staff who were his age welcomed him wholeheartedly into their activities—activities that largely fell on weekends when he should be attending church.

I wrote him long letters, reminding him that testimonies were fragile and needed constant spiritual replenishing. I urged him to attend his meetings, emphasizing that church was a place to partake of the sacrament and to worship; and, although it would be nice to have friends there, the important thing was to be where he was supposed to be on the Sabbath. More than once Kay called his bishop, urging him to assign Lee home teachers and to alert the elders quorum president to the need for fellowshipping. Even our ward bishop called him, but nothing happened.

As I walked the streets that night, I longed to place the responsibility of Lee's inactivity on a too-busy bishop and a complacent ward. But I couldn't. Lee was an adult and responsible for his own choices. That made it even harder to bear.

Lee had great love and respect for our bishop, and that night he sought Bishop Ward's guidance. I was waiting for him when he came home shortly before midnight, and once more we talked long into the night. He was in great mental anguish. He wanted to believe as his family believed and to have assurance of things which, until now, he had always believed; but his heart was plagued with doubts. Was God a reality or, as some of his friends maintained, a mythical crutch we used to get through the trials and misfortunes of life? And, if there was a God, did He really care what label we put on ourselves or what organizational structure we belonged to as long as we didn't lie, steal, cheat, or hurt other people? I knew that he must resolve those questions, along with others that were troubling him, by himself. I could only bear testimony to him of that which I believed and pray that the Lord would help him believe, too.

Armed with his scriptures and patriarchal blessing, Lee left the next morning for the cabin in McCall where he would spend the next few days alone, praying and pondering. I had never felt more helpless.

Lee was pale and exhausted when he returned home. He said he knew there was a God and that the gospel was true. However, he still had some things to work out, and it would take time. He didn't want us to hurry him. That night I knelt by my bed and gave grateful thanks.

Lee had planned on moving back to Boise; but while he was in McCall, word came from the National Cystic Fibrosis Foundation that he had been accepted for an accounting internship in Bethesda, Maryland, beginning the middle of June. Rather than move twice, he would return to Salt Lake until time to move to Maryland. Three times he had applied for that internship; twice he had been turned down. Now, at the very time when he needed the spiritual support of family and friends the most, he had been accepted. How ironic!

In June, Kay and I drove to Salt Lake to spend a few days with him before he left for Maryland. While Lee and I cleaned the now-empty apartment, he talked about Heidi, a girl who worked in Kristy's office and whom he had been dating. "I worried about how to tell her I had C/F," he admitted. "Mostly, I guess, because it's the first time I've had to tell someone who mattered a lot to me. Before, they either already knew, or someone soon told them. Heidi is special, though, and I felt I should be the one to tell her. It took me a while to lead into it, but on about our fourth date I finally told her."

"What did she say?" I asked, standing on top of a stool and stretching to clean a top shelf.

Lee took the cloth from my hand. "Here, let me do that. You're going to break your neck. Actually, she really didn't say much," he answered, giving the shelf a light once-over. "Just kinda cried and said it wasn't fair. That was about it. She's a tender-hearted girl." He dropped the cloth back into the sudsy water. "But Kristy told me that the next day she went into her office, closed the door, and started to cry. That started Kristy crying, and I guess they had a good boo-hoo together. Then she asked Kristy a lot of questions about C/F.

"We've really hit it off well, but she's young and has her whole life ahead of her. Probably, the minute I'm on the plane, I'll be history and she'll be out with someone else," he added philosophically.

"Will that bother you?" I asked. He shrugged and didn't answer. I had the feeling that it would.

Two days later, Pat, Steve, Kay, his doctor friend, Dr. Burch, and I watched him board the plane to Maryland, his head full of dreams that the internship would turn into a full-time career.

Sunday, June 18, 1989—Letter from Lee in Maryland:

"I made it! The apartment is very nice—two bedrooms with a bathroom for each. The complex is quite large, probably 200-300 tenants with a large pool. The office is about fifteen miles away.

"My roommate is twenty-two, a graduate student in computer science—a brain. Mom, you needn't have nagged me to get a shorter haircut. His hair is in a pony tail that hangs way down his back, and he has a mustache and goatee. He's friendly and personable, and we're hitting it off fine.

"The interns are a fun group, even the two guys who are yuppies right down to their polo shirts! It's amazing, however, how little some of them seem to know about C/F and how casual they are about their care. The majority don't have access to a clinic like Salt Lake, and I get the feeling they have no support group of C/F friends and medical personnel. I feel fortunate to be associated with the Salt Lake Clinic and its family feeling.

"Well, we're all getting together and cook some food so I will close. Take care, and I love you both. See you at the end of the summer. Love, Lee."

Saturday, June 24, 1989—Letter from Lee:

"The first week at work went okay. I'll work in the unrestricted funds for four weeks and then in restricted funds the last four weeks.

"We get home from work close to 7:00 p.m., fix dinner, watch a little TV, do a treatment and then go to bed. The days fly by.

"I called James, and he's not well. He told me he had started saying his goodbyes. He said he'd try to hold on for a while longer, but he's really tired of fighting. We couldn't bring ourselves to say goodbye over the phone. Afterward, I called Heidi and asked her to visit him for me."

Tuesday, July 4, 1989—Letter from Lee:

"Well, Mom, how does it feel to be retired after working so many years? Hope you are enjoying it.

"Today was quite an experience. We had the day off and took the Metro into D.C. It rained until almost time for the fireworks. Everyone got soaked, with or without an umbrella. We ducked in and out of buildings and exhibits, and in between downpours we walked to the Capitol where the National Symphony was playing and hung out in front of the Capitol at the reflecting pools, listening to the music and watching the people go by. From there, we walked down to the Lincoln Memorial; but most of the time we visited the Science Smithsonian, which was really something. Nephew Eddy would have loved it!

"When the rain had pretty much stopped, we picked our plot in the grassy area between the Capitol and the Lincoln Memorial. The fireworks exploded just above the monument and were fantastic. The finale had more explosions than McCall's whole show!

"The Metro ride back was an experience in itself. Imagine 200,000-300,000 people in one subway station trying to get home. The crowd was jammed in so tight that when the car stopped, I was literally lifted off the ground and carried for about six feet. Miraculously, all four of our group made it. I love it here. Health good. Not to worry! Love, Lee."

Lee called late the night of July 7 to tell us that James had died the morning before. He talked for a long time, often disjointedly, while I listened quietly.

"Peggy called me from the clinic day before yesterday and said they were starting the narcotic drip. As soon as she hung up, I went into an empty office and called him. He was confused and tired, somewhat delirious at times; but he knew who I was. He kept repeating my name, and we said our goodbyes.

"No matter how much you prepare for it, when it happens it's still a shock. We were as close as brothers. I guess when you experience a lot of the same things, you become close in a way that's difficult to explain. It'll be hard not having him there when I go back.

"I think James knew before I left Salt Lake that this would be his last hospital stay, because he talked a lot about dying. I think what scared him the most was that it might happen when he was alone. I'm glad his family was with him when he went, especially his grandmother. He lived with her in Moab, and they were extremely close, more like mother and son than grandmother and grandson.

"James and I were of the same mindset about dying. It wasn't that we were afraid of what happens after we die, but of the way we were going to die. C/F is not the easiest way to go, and I think if we had our choice about dying it would be quick and without knowing anything about it, like a car crash. From what I understand from those with him at the clinic, though, the narcotic drip helped him. I hope so.

"James and I used to talk, too, about not wanting to be mixed up and irrational at the end. The doctors say that's part of what happens, though. When that carbon dioxide builds up and starts screwing up your brain, you pretty much lose rational thought, and that's one thing James and I dreaded having happen to us. We wanted to remain in control until it was over. When I talked with James Wednesday, he was a little mixed up, but I'm sure he knew who I was because he kept saying my name.

"I'm glad Dr. Taylor was in charge at the end because she was a good friend of his and, I understand, helped him keep his dignity by keeping non-essential people and visitors, except for family, out of his room. She knew how both of us felt about dying with dignity."

After he hung up, I locked myself in the bathroom and turned on the bath water. I didn't want Kay to hear me crying.

When Lee called again two weeks later, he was, of course, still in pain over James' death. However, much of his conversation centered around a prospective job offer from the Foundation. Two supervisors had already informally sounded him out about working for them once his internship was completed. When I asked how he'd responded, he said, "I told them that all I needed was time to fly back to Salt Lake, throw my belongings in the back of my truck, and I'd be on my way."

Just four days after his call, Lee was back in Salt Lake. The Cystic Fibrosis Foundation had decided to discontinue the young adult internship programs until they had more information about the potential for cross-infection of C/F individuals with pseudomonas cepacia.* As Lee gave us the details leading up to the closure of the internship program, it was clear that he was devastated, and I wondered if he would be able to bounce back from this latest blow.

In August, we held our family reunion at McCall. As usual, in the evenings the cabin walls reverberated with the voices and

---

*Scientists have now concluded that person-to-person contact in a hospital setting and other intensive contact between C/F individuals can be a means of transmitting pseudomonas cepacia.

antics of exuberant grandchildren. Kay fled to the beach on the pretense of making sure the boats were secure; and Lee, easily fatigued in the higher altitude, bedded down early in his sleeping bag in the back of his pickup, a long extension cord running from the cabin to his oxygen concentrator. The smaller children looked at his accommodations with envious eyes and begged their parents to let them sleep under the stars with Uncle Lee rather than in the "boring" cabin or in "dumb" tents with their parents. "He has all the fun," a little one muttered.

"Yeah," agreed his little cousin. "But I'd hate to breathe that special air he breathes through that mask. I smelled it once, and it stinks."

On August 25, 1989, the news that the C/F gene had been discovered hit the newspapers. Our local C/F staff jubilantly predicted the end of C/F within four or five years at the most. Considering Lee's health, even four or five years seemed an eternity. Perhaps that's why when I told Dr. Venning, he replied glumly, "That doesn't help Lee a damn bit."

Wednesday, November 22, 1989—Entry from Lee's Journal:

"I've been living in the Sunburst Apartment Complex in West Valley City a week now and quite enjoy it. I have a small studio apartment with modern furniture and modern appliances. It's well-lit and sports a much better color scheme than the green carpets and rust furniture of my old apartment in downtown Salt Lake. This apartment is closer to Steve and Kristy, and I like that.

"I've decided this will be my last move for a long time. I don't enjoy moving anymore. My sixteen-day stay in the hospital in October nearly wiped me out, and it gets harder and harder to pack and unpack, even with all the help I've had. I'm glad for friends and family that help me out when I need it, and I find I'm needing it more and more often. In the meantime, I'm working when I can for temporary job services and dating Heidi."

—1990—

In February, Lee's doctor removed the central line in his arm and surgically implanted a permanent catheter called a Port-A-Cath in a major vein leading to the heart. It was placed under the skin in the right pectoral region, and when I first saw the round bulge, it reminded me of the voice boxes they used to put in dolls when I was a little girl.

When Kay and I visited Lee again in April, we were shocked by his appearance. Even on oxygen, he was cyanotic. "I'm not bouncing back like I used to," he observed bluntly. "Maybe it's time I started thinking about moving back home, at least until I get my strength back."

"Why don't you come home with us now?" I urged. "We can come after your belongings later."

He shook his head. "Remember me telling you about Steve Braddock, one of my doctors? He's getting married next weekend in Missouri, and he's asked me to be in his wedding party. With all the friends he has, it's quite an honor," he said, looking smug. "As soon as I get back, I'll check into the hospital for a couple of weeks and get cleaned out. Then we'll see."

"You sound like you should be in the hospital now instead of flying to Missouri. I'm sure Dr. Braddock doesn't want you to take chances with your health."

"I'll be okay. The doc put me on septra the other day, and by Friday I'll be feeling better. Besides, Steve will keep an eye on me the weekend of the wedding."

"Right," I replied dryly. "He can keep one eye on you and one eye on his bride!"

Lee was still dragging the next morning, but he needed a new pair of pants so I took him to the mall. When he told the clerk the pants needed to be rugged enough to wear mountain biking and still be comfortable enough to wear in the hospital, she gave us a questioning look. I shrugged. Luckily, the first pair he tried on fit. Even that much exertion exhausted him.

He was lying on his bed soaking up oxygen when the phone rang. It was Kristy. She had heard about a job opening at the University of Utah. It was in accounting and was only part-time. If Lee was interested, he would need to get his resume in the next day. Lee's eyes lit up. Of course he was interested! This would be the perfect job. He would hand-deliver his resume tomorrow on the way to the hospital to get his Port-A-Cath flushed. It was as if the oxygen cannula in his nose, the debilitating cough, and his deteriorating lungs didn't exist.

I looked at him and my heart broke. I saw what Lee refused to see—a terribly ill young man, far too incapacitated to hold down a job. Swallowing the lump in my throat, I wished him good luck.

As soon as he returned from Dr. Braddock's wedding, he checked into the hospital and called us. He'd had a grand time and was happy he'd gone. As for the accounting job at the University of Utah, he hadn't heard back so he supposed he wasn't in the running. No, he hadn't decided exactly when he would be coming home to live. Probably in late summer, depending on his health.

In May, I called and wished him a happy 27th birthday. He was going to dinner at Steve's and Kristy's to celebrate his "day of birthing." In a voice crackling with excitement, he said he and some friends were making plans to float a sixteen-mile stretch of the Snake River in Wyoming. They would stay in Jackson, raft the river, and enjoy the Tetons for a weekend.

This was the same boy who had been discharged from the hospital only four days before, and who, less than a month earlier, could scarcely walk without oxygen. Appalled, I asked, "What do your doctors say about that?"

"They said they wished they could go, too, and to have fun," he answered airily.

Tuesday, July 3, 1990—Letter from Lee:

"About a dozen people went on the river trip, and we had a great time. Because of the high runoff, we went with an experienced runner. It rained most of the trip, but the river gear helped. Anyway, once we hit the white water, dryness was of no concern. Those up in front had the best (and the wettest) ride. I was lucky and was able to position myself there. It was a completely new experience for me, and I found the whole thing most invigorating. You should try it sometime!

"And, Mom, I'm okay. I lost a few pounds because of three days without my nighttime feedings and my oxygen, but other than that I'm none the worse for the trip. As I've told you before, you worry too much!"

During our next trip to Salt Lake, I had a private talk with one of his doctors. The doctor was candid. In essence, he said that Lee had deteriorated rapidly during the past two years and was now severely handicapped. The lung damage was irreversible; and even if by some miracle the control for C/F were discovered immediately, it would be too late for him. His airways were too severely damaged.

In a strangled voice, I asked the question I'd vowed never to ask. "How much time has he left?"

The doctor's answer was slow in coming, and when it came it was uttered with unspeakable sadness. "No one knows for certain, of course; a few months, certainly less than a year. It depends on many factors. Lee is a fighter, but—." His voice trailed off.

"There has to be *something* we can do," I cried. "What about a double lung transplant or a heart-lungs transplant? I've read that several C/F patients have had successful heart-lungs transplants."

He was sorry. They had already made inquiries along that line. Lee had lost any option he might have had for a transplantation when he suffered the pneumothorax in 1987. The thoracotomy, which had saved his life at the time, now prevented him from being considered as a transplant candidate. "Thoracotomy aside," the doctor continued, "Lee has two other contraindications to transplant surgery—pseudomonas cepacia and diabetes mellitus. Those alone could disqualify him."

"How much of this does he know?" I asked.

He skirted the question by saying, "Lee is extremely knowledgeable about cystic fibrosis and about his own care, often to the consternation of an inexperienced intern. He knows that transplantation isn't an option and that he's going downhill rapidly. He tries to conceal it, but there are times in the hospital when we know he's extremely depressed. Between hospitalizations he pushes himself, trying to gain back the ground he's lost, as if by sheer willpower he can reverse the progress of the disease. Of course he can't, but he never quits trying. He's a courageous young man. You can be proud of him."

During the year, it became financially necessary for us to sell our cabin, and in August we held our first family reunion without it. I was worried that it wouldn't be fun, especially for the grandchildren. I needn't have been concerned. I should have known that it wasn't the lake and the cabin that made our reunions fun. It was the getting together. Oh, there were a few teary eyes when someone referred to McCall or the cabin; but as one little granddaughter confided to her favorite cousin, "I don't care where we are, as long as me and you are together."

As always, the reunion ended all too quickly; and before we knew it, parents were rounding up their children to go home. While Sylvia made certain that their youngsters took advantage of the bathroom facilities one last time, Stan motioned that he wanted to speak to me privately. We went upstairs, and he closed the den door.

Walking over to the window, he stared outside. A doer rather than a talker, Stan often found it difficult to express himself in words. I waited. I hadn't missed the anxious way he'd watched Lee all weekend, and I dreaded what was coming. At last, he spoke. "Lee's getting much worse, isn't he?" he stated more than asked. Without waiting for an answer, he continued, "When I finished water skiing at the reservoir Friday, he asked me to pull him. You know how fussy he is when he skis, wanting to be pulled at exactly his speed and all that. Well, I started out at his usual speed, and he kept motioning for me to slow down. Then, instead of jumping the wake or leaning over to make a rooster tail, he just let the boat pull him along. He'd only skied a few minutes when he let go of the rope and let himself sink into the water. When I brought the boat around, he was too exhausted to climb up the ladder. I had to jump in and help him. Once in the boat, he coughed harder than I've ever heard him cough before, and then he spit out a mouthful of blood. I guess I looked scared because he shrugged and said he did that sometimes, that it didn't mean anything.

"The next day when we played volleyball, he only played for a couple of minutes. I followed him into the house, and he was sitting hunched over on the couch, breathing hard. When I asked him how he was, he said he was okay, just out of breath, probably needed to go into the hospital and get cleaned out. It was nothing to worry about. Does he really only need to get 'cleaned out' like he says, or is this the way he's going to be from now on?" he demanded, blinking hard.

My first impulse was to protect him, to tell him that this was only one more down in twenty-seven years of ups and downs, that the cure was just around the corner, and that all we had to do was hang on. But he deserved to know the truth, and I told him the doctor's prognosis. Tears filled his eyes, and when I finished we put our arms around each other and stood silently comforting each other until a child's voice from downstairs called out that everyone was waiting in the car. It was time for him to go. When he gave Lee an extra tight hug as he left, no one noticed except me.

Friday, August 10, 1990—Letter from Lee:

"I had a good time at the reunion. Good food, weather and company. Not much to say in this letter because it was all said at the reunion. I still plan on moving back to Boise next month. Except for Heidi, I don't have any really close friends here now. They've either died or moved away. Love from #7."

But he didn't move home. Instead he moved to Seattle, Washington. For several months, Reed Nokleby, a childhood friend who now lived in Seattle, had urged him to move there and share an apartment with him and another friend.

When it first came up, Lee didn't give it much thought. He'd already decided to come home. I was elated because, in spite of his doctor's prognosis, I still clung to the hope that once he was home we could turn his condition around as we'd done so many times before. If we failed, at least I would have these last precious months with him to treasure.

I was visiting Lee in the Salt Lake hospital when he told me he had decided to move to Seattle for at least a few months before coming home to stay. In spite of my efforts to conceal it, the pain in my heart must have shown on my face because he added softly, "Now, Mom, I'm going to be okay, and Reed needs me right now. He really does."

In October, pulling a small U-Haul that contained all his worldly possessions, he started his move from Salt Lake to Seattle. He almost didn't make it. Several miles outside of Snowville, Utah, his truck broke down. Snowville is a farming community consisting largely of a truckstop, a small garage, a cafe, and an old motel. Although the calendar still said fall, Snowville was living up to its name, and already the surrounding hills had a dusting of snow. The temperature was near freezing.

Lee's teeth were chattering when he called us from the pay phone outside the garage. "I broke down too far from here to make it in on foot," he explained, "and no one would stop so I hiked over to a farm house. It was quite a long ways, but I was able to make it and called a tow truck. I'm at a garage now, but it's closed so I'll have to stay here tonight. Dad, do you think I should get the truck fixed here or have it towed into Burley where there are more garages?"

Every few words were punctuated by coughing followed by heavy breathing. Listening, I burst out, "Stop talking about the stupid truck and get out of the cold. You can decide that later."

"Mom's right," Kay agreed. "Get a lift to the motel and hole up for the night. We'll decide about the truck in the morning."

"I don't see anyone around to hitch a ride with, but the motel isn't far. I can make it if I leave my bag and everything in the truck."

Another grinding coughing spell made conversation impossible. When it was over, I demanded, "Lee, you call us the minute you walk into that motel room. I want to be sure you get there all right." He felt that was a bit much, but he promised.

Silently, Kay and I sat by the phone, listening to the clock tick off the minutes—five, ten, fifteen. Another five minutes passed, and then another. Why didn't he call? Dozens of possibilities rushed through my mind, all of them terrifying. "I'll give him five more minutes," I announced grimly, "then I'm calling the Snowville police. For all we know, that motel could be boarded up, and he can't make it back to the truck stop. The way he sounded, he may even be having another pneumothorax." For once, Kay didn't tell me I was blowing everything out of proportion.

Four minutes later, the phone rang. He was in his room. He was sorry it took him so long to call, but the motel was farther away than he'd thought; and, too, he'd been facing a cold wind and had had to stop and rest every few feet. He wished there had been a way to get his concentrator to the motel, because he could use some oxygen; but he was lying down and feeling better. He would call us as soon as he found out about the truck in the morning. Not to worry, he was okay.

In spite of being told not to worry, it was a long night, and we were relieved when he called the next morning. He was getting the truck fixed there, but it would be late afternoon before it was ready. We weren't to expect him until very late because he would have to drive slowly. The wind was gusting, and he didn't want it to tip over the U-Haul. We were to go to bed and not worry!

It was nearly morning before we heard the pickup stop in front of the house and the truck door slam. We rushed out to help him carry in his suitcase. Everything else could wait until morning. Exhausted, he turned on the concentrator we kept ready for him in his room and fell into bed. It was one of the few times in his life that he'd gone to bed without a drainage.

Kay wanted to go with him on the last leg of his trip to Seattle and fly back, but Lee insisted he would be fine. He figured that everything that could go wrong with the truck had already gone wrong.

Just before he left, he asked his dad for a father's blessing, the first he'd requested in a long time. Afterward, father and son embraced in a fierce hug. My cheeks were not the only damp ones in the room.

Friday, October 12, 1990—Letter from Lee:

"I'm finally here. What a nightmare the first leg of the trip was, but we won't dwell on that! The trip from Boise to Seattle is 500 miles and took ten hours. It was slow because of the high winds in central Washington, but uneventful.

"The apartment has three bedrooms, two bathrooms, and a fireplace. We are located in south Seattle, technically Tukwila. Right now, I'm just trying to find my way around and get established. This is a confusing place—water everywhere. Can't keep my north and south straight.

"Yes, Mom, I've called the C/F Center and have an appointment for Friday. Not to worry; I'm okay."

Lee came home Thanksgiving week, and spent Thanksgiving with the family in Orem at Pat's and Robert's home. He was coughing hard and had lost more weight in spite of the nighttime feedings and oxygen. He shrugged it off and said that as soon as he got back to Seattle he was going to check into the hospital and get cleaned out again.

The week before Christmas, he came home again. He had spent fifteen days in the hospital, but he was still coughing and had lost more weight. He was going downhill rapidly.

On Christmas morning, I was up long before Kay and Lee stirred. There was much to do, and the children and grandchildren would soon be arriving to open their gifts and enjoy Christmas dinner. With the turkey stuffed and in the oven, jello salads setting up in the refrigerator, and orange rolls put out to raise, I left the kitchen and stood at the living room window, looking out at the frozen snow drifted high in the yard. Across the street, the neighbors' Christmas tree blazed into life, and there was six-year-old David in the window, hopping from one foot to the other, beside himself with excitement.

At the sight, memories of Christmases past flooded over me— memories of little daughters, eyes aglow with excitement, hugging precious new dolls while their little brothers tumbled over each other in their eagerness to see what Santa had left. Standing there, reliving those wonderfully hectic mornings, I gradually became aware of Lee standing beside me. As if reading my mind, he said, "Christmas mornings are different now, aren't they, Mom? Do you remember how Dad would come downstairs in his bright red Christmas vest and red bow tie, and put Sousa's 'Stars and Stripes Forever' on the record player to get us up? Then he'd hand out the presents one at a time, and we'd all have to wait until that present was opened and admired before he'd hand out the next. I was always glad that he started with the youngest kid first. I don't think I could have stood getting my present last like Mary. Speaking of presents, I see a few under the tree with my name on them! Let's put Sousa on and get Dad up."

As he turned to the record cabinet, he gave me a squeeze and said, "I've had a good life, Mom. Thanks."

I knew then that he knew this would be his last Christmas.

—1991—

Lee made a quick visit to family and friends in the Salt Lake area during the Christmas holidays, and before returning to Seattle he told us about his trip.

"Did I tell you that Charlie has been accepted for a double lung transplant by a surgeon in St. Louis?" he asked, his voice pleased. "His grandmother will drive him, and they'll live in an apartment until donor lungs become available. Charlie's really excited. He figures if the operation works, he'll have it made."

I shot a glance at him. His face reflected pleasure for his friend, nothing more. If he were sorry that he wasn't eligible for transplantation, he gave no hint.

After spending two weeks in the hospital at the University of Washington Medical Center in February, he came home again. He didn't care for some of the resident doctors (he claimed that he knew more about C/F than they did), but he had nothing but praise for Dr. Moira Aitken, his primary C/F physician. "She knows what she's doing," he said. He also volunteered that he enjoyed his church ward, and that Bishop Nelson was "a great guy."

That afternoon and evening he sat cross-legged on the floor of his room, sorting through his belongings. I noted uneasily that formerly treasured memorabilia received only a cursory glance before being tossed into a large discard box. Without being told, I knew he was putting his things in order; and suddenly every scrap of paper, every worn-out bit of clothing, everything that had been even remotely a part of his life was precious to me. After he was asleep, I retrieved the throw-away box with its contents and secreted it in my room.

During March, Lee spent more time in the hospital than he

spent out. We urged him to come home, but he said Dr. Aitken was still hopeful that she could turn him around. He thought he should stay put. When his dad told him we were coming up, he asked us to wait until he was out of the hospital.

Early one morning in April, he called and said that Dr. Aitken had just left his room. She had asked him how he'd feel about applying for a double lung transplantation at the same St. Louis hospital where Charlie was waiting for his. She thought they might accept him. I caught my breath in surprise. "What did you say?" I asked.

"I said I'd have to think about it. Even if the operation was successful, in a year or two C/F would wreck the new lungs, and I'd be back to square one. Maybe I'm just tired, but right now it doesn't seem worth it. What do you think I should do, Mom?"

The mere possibility of his being accepted for transplantation sent renewed hope surging through my body. However, it was immediately replaced by misgivings. In spite of Dr. Aitken's optimism, Lee's acceptance was unlikely. Was it fair to build up his hopes again? Hadn't he been jerked around enough? Even if he was by some miracle accepted into the program, it would mean relocating to St. Louis and waiting for donor lungs to become available, a wait that could well be six months or longer. Could he possibly hang on that long? It was doubtful. What a tragedy for him to spend the few remaining months of his life far from home, waiting for lungs that wouldn't come in time.

On the other hand, suppose he was accepted and the operation was a success? Researchers were rapidly closing in on gene therapy, and the additional years could make the difference between life and death. Dared we not take the chance, however unlikely it sounded?

Taking a deep breath, I replied, "Son, you're the one who in the end will have to make the decision. But I don't see that you have anything to lose by applying. Applying doesn't mean the decision is chiseled in stone."

"For me, applying will mean it's chiseled in stone," he corrected. "If I apply and am accepted, I'll go for it. I only want to make up my mind once."

We talked for a few more minutes, and then, sounding more positive, he said, "I'm going to give Charlie a call in St. Louis and ask him some questions. As I think about it, maybe applying wouldn't be such a bad idea. I could use some additional good years."

Although sensitivity tests indicated that Lee's pseudomonas cepacia was resistant to all antibiotics, he was, nevertheless, on aggressive antibiotic therapy. In order to counteract his continuing weight loss, his nocturnal tube feedings were changed from Pulmocare to a higher-density, higher-calorie nutrient. This nutrient, together with the cepacia infection, caused his diabetes to flair out of control. It seemed that trying to put out one fire only started a dozen more.

On the chance that a sinus infection was contributing to his condition, both of his maxillary sinuses were tapped, drained, and irrigated. He was in a great deal of pain and very angry when I phoned him that afternoon. "I told them I didn't want it done, but they kept at me until I gave in," he said furiously. "It didn't accomplish a thing except to give me a ton of unnecessary pain."

They had changed him back to Pulmocare feedings, but his glucose was still over five hundred. However, the prednisone was reducing the inflammation in his lungs and making it easier to breathe.

"What about the cepacia? Are the antibiotics bringing it under control?" I asked.

He hesitated, and I knew he was deciding how much to tell me. I mentally braced myself. "Dr. Aitken had a long talk with me yesterday," he said. "The cepacia isn't responding to any of the antibiotics; and, to use her words, 'that is a very poor prognostic sign'." He must have heard my swift intake of breath because he continued gently, "Mom, we've both known this day would come, and now it's here. I'm not going to get well. I'm coming home."

No matter how long and hard I cried, the pain didn't dissolve.

Unable to accept that nothing more could be done, I called Dr. Aitken. In a voice filled with compassion she said, "Some time ago Lee told me he was returning to Boise, and I asked him to give me a month to try and turn his condition around. He agreed, and during that time we've tried everything. Now he wants to return home, which I feel is a mature and correct decision. He needs to be with his family.

"The only thing left is lung transplantation," she continued, "and he seems uncharacteristically hesitant about that. Do you know why?"

"As far as I know, there are at least two reasons," I answered. "One is that he doesn't think he would be accepted; and the other is that even if he was, and the operation was a success, in a year or two the new lungs would be as bad as the ones he has now."

"Where did he get an idea like that?" she cried. "If the operation is successful, the new lungs should last for many years. I'll clear that up with him this afternoon."

Before Lee was released from the hospital, he and Dr. Aitken completed papers requesting that he be considered for a double lung transplantation. Dr. Aitken was pleased when she called us with Lee's decision. "For the first time, he smiled and joked with me," she said. "He's definitely made the correct decision for him. He may not be accepted into the program, but he'll know that he's now tried everything possible. He'll never wonder if he gave up too soon."

It was difficult for me to bring up my next concern. When a loved one's life is involved, there is something obscene about admitting, even to oneself, that money, or lack thereof, enters into the picture. However, obscene or not, unless the money was paid up front, there would be no operation. Because they considered lung transplantations experimental, Lee's insurance carriers refused coverage. Kay and I would need to come up with an initial $250,000 for the transplant, plus Lee's and my relocation expenses and numerous other costs such as his evaluation, our airfare, and so forth. We were talking at least $300,000, and probably much more. Kay had added up our assets, and even after liquidating everything we could, we would be short. Dr. Aitken needed to know this before proceeding further.

When I told her of our situation, she replied, "You're looking too far ahead, Mrs. Belnap. There's still much to do, and we need to take this one step at a time. Don't worry about the money at this point."

"The problem won't go away by not worrying about it," I answered. In spite of myself, my voice broke. "I'm sorry," I whispered. "It's just that I don't think I could stand it if everything were in place, and at the last minute I had to tell Lee the operation was off because his parents couldn't come up with the money."

"If he's eligible for the transplantation, he'll have it," she announced grimly. "I'm a fighter, and I've done this before. There are ways. Don't worry." Even while I promised that I wouldn't worry, I knew I was making a promise I couldn't keep.

May 10 was Lee's twenty-eighth birthday; but there was no birthday cake, no laughing crowd of family and friends, no happy grin and blowing out of candles. Instead, it was a somber day, with Kay and Roger preparing to fly to Seattle early the next morning to bring Lee's belongings home in his truck.

Irene and I would meet him at the airport with oxygen and a wheelchair. The airline would supply the oxygen for the short flight home.

My personal journal entries tell the rest of the story.

Saturday, May 11, 1991:

Lee is home. Irene and I met him at the airport this morning. He had warned me that he looked bad and not to be shocked when I saw him. Still, I wasn't prepared. Neither was Irene. If Lee saw her lips quiver when we helped him into the wheelchair, he gave no sign. He simply said, "Thanks for coming after me. I'm glad to be home."

Thursday, May 16, 1991:

Lee ran into serious trouble this morning, and we rushed him to Dr. Merrick's office. Even on oxygen, he was extremely short of breath and cyanotic before we got him there. It had been almost three years since Dr. Merrick had seen him, and even his practiced professional mask couldn't disguise his initial shock when he saw Lee's skeletal form sitting in the wheelchair in his office.

He quickly reviewed Lee's file, penning in notes as Lee brought him up to date. When Lee mentioned he had applied for lung transplantation, the doctor looked up, surprised. Lee caught his look and observed wryly, "I don't think I'll be accepted, but at this point, I don't see that I have anything to lose by applying."

Dr. Merrick nodded and turned back to his file. "I've a note here, Lee, that states you don't want CPR or to be put on any kind of life support. Do you still feel that way?"

Lee nodded his head. "I still feel that way."

Dr. Merrick duly noted it on his chart. I was glad that neither he nor Lee looked at me. I knew my face reflected the sickness in my heart.

A thorough examination followed, and finally Dr. Merrick brought him back to his office. "Lee," he said, "I know this looks bad, and you have to be discouraged. But I'm not giving up, and I don't want you to, either. I'm going to hospitalize you and start tobra and fortaz intravenously. Also, we'll begin steroid injections. The steroids will reduce the swelling in your lungs and make you more comfortable. At least for now, we'll keep the remainder of your medications the same. I'll be over later to take your blood gases."

With Lee in the hospital, Kay and I were going to cancel the birthday party we'd planned for him. However, when I leaned over to kiss him goodnight, he whispered, "Tell the out-of-town families to come as planned for the weekend. I'm not up to much company, but I'd like a few minutes alone with each of my brothers and sisters."

Tonight I called the six children. I tried to keep my voice steady, but still there were tears. Without being told, they knew Lee wanted to tell them goodbye.

Friday, May 17, 1991:

Stan was the first of the children to visit Lee. He came back looking drained, his eyes red and swollen; and I knew he had stopped somewhere on the way home to cry. "Lee's our same old Lee, though," he said, lips twisting slightly. "When he finished with what he had to say, he heaved a big sigh and grunted, 'Well, that's over. Now, if I make it another year or so, don't expect another talk. You've had it!'"

The word has quickly circulated through the ward that Lee is in the hospital, and several ward members have stuck their heads in to welcome him home and to tell him their prayers are with him. His room is crowded with equipment, and his shortness of breath makes speaking exhausting. Recognizing this, many simply wave at him from the door. The support of our ward overwhelms us.

Lee requested that he be given a blessing, and tonight Kay, Stan, Steve, and Roger laid their hands upon his head, and in that hushed hospital room, Steve gave his beloved brother a priesthood blessing. Tears flowed as the Spirit of the Lord filled the room. The blessing was unlike any other Lee had received. The promises made were not of recovery in this life, but of blessings awaiting him on the other side of the veil.

Saturday, May 18, 1991:

Tonight the adults of the family celebrated Lee's birthday of last week in his hospital room with presents and a birthday cake inscribed, "Happy Birthday, #7." There were no candles on the cake. Lori had thoughtfully omitted them, knowing that Lee could not blow even one out. With forced gaiety we watched him open his gifts, carefully avoiding each other's eyes lest our cheerful veneer crack under the weight of knowing this was his last birthday.

There was genuine merriment, however, when he opened the present from Mary and Dee. It was a large, monster-shaped horn that squawked dreadfully when squeezed. Because it was tiring for him to talk, Lee had fallen into the practice of snapping his fingers to get my attention and then pointing at what he wanted. This was not lost on his brothers and sisters, who remembered when requests not prefaced with a "please" were, for the most part, ignored by their mother. Now, here she was, leaping to attention at the mere snap of her youngest's fingers! Mary explained, "Now all you need to do, Lee, is squeeze on this, and you can summon Mom from any room in the house!"

Tuesday, May 21, 1991:

Today, after consulting with Dr. Thomas Coffman, an infectious disease specialist, Dr. Merrick discontinued the fortaz and tobramycin and began massive doses of Bactrim IV in an attempt to control the cepacia.

Carol Wood, the C/F Clinic Coordinator in Salt Lake, called this afternoon and brightened our day when she said that Charlie Stockdale has received his new lungs and is in stable condition. It wasn't until Lee said how pleased he was for Charlie that I realized I had unconsciously let go of any hope for a transplant for Lee.

Wednesday, May 22, 1991:

This morning, one of the nurses beckoned me from Lee's room and told me that Dr. Merrick wanted me to call him from a room other than Lee's. She took me to an empty one, gave my hand a squeeze, and walked out, closing the door softly behind her. Her solicitous eyes had told me more than she'd intended, and for a few minutes I stood staring down at the phone, not wanting to pick it up. As long as the words weren't actually spoken, I was safe. I could still pretend that Lee was going to live.

Biting deep into my lower lip to stay its trembling, I dialed the doctor's number; within seconds he was on the phone. The message was brief. Lee could not survive much longer.

I don't know how long I stood frozen in that empty room, unable to breathe for the suffocating pain, waves of blackness washing over me. After a while, there came a tentative rap on the door, and a soft voice called out, "Mrs. Belnap, are you all right?"

I opened the door and walked into a pair of waiting arms.

Friday, May 24, 1991:

Today Lee talked for the first time about his fears. "I've never been this sick before," he said, his blue-nailed fingers absently picking at the white sheet, "not even when I had the pneumothorax. Funny, I used to get mad at the nurses when they'd forget and leave my door open during the night. Now I'm uneasy when they close it." His lips quivered, and he quit speaking. Never before had he looked more fragile or childlike than at that vulnerable moment. Tears burned my eyes, and I leaned over and kissed his feverish forehead.

For a long time he lay quietly against his pillows, his eyes closed, his hand clasped tightly in mine. Finally he said, "Sorry, Mom. I'm not all that bad. I do have some questions to ask Dr. Merrick when he comes in, though, if you don't mind jotting them down." I rummaged around in my purse and came up with pen and paper. He had me write down several medical questions before he voiced the one that was preying on his mind.

"I know C/F isn't the most pleasant way to go," he said matter-of-factly, "and I remember Dr. Taylor telling me that toward the end they gave James something to make him more comfortable. I'd like to know Dr. Merrick's feelings about that. I'm not nervous about what happens to me after I die—the hard part is getting from here to there."

When the doctor came by on his rounds, I gave him Lee's questions. He was in a hurry and said he'd get back to us.

Until Lee told me, I had no idea he was uneasy at night, and I'm angry at myself for being so obtuse. But he'll never be alone at night again. This afternoon, a nurse and I dragged an ancient reclining chair into his room and wedged it between his bed and the window seat. It's in so tight that I have to crawl over the foot rest to get in and out, but that's good because I'm within touching distance of him.

I expected Lee to demur when I told him I'd sleep better if I could stay nights with him. Instead, he nodded his head, gave me a tremulous smile, and said, "You're a good mom."

Sunday, May 26, 1991:

Lee's breathing became so labored during the night that the nurse called Dr. Merrick at home; shortly afterward, an inhalation therapist came into the room. He gave Lee a treatment, increased his oxygen, and, after some experimenting, replaced the nasal cannula with a snug-fitting oxygen mask. For a few hours, Lee breathed more easily.

However, about 7:00 this morning, he threw his arm over his head and arched his back just as he had years before when Dr. Kane sclerosed his lung. His face turned blue, and his nails dug into the pillows propped behind him. I screamed for a nurse and scrambled off the recliner. By the time the nurse reached us, Lee had caught his breath. When he could speak, he said that it wasn't a plug. His chest muscles had simply quit working.

Toward noon, Dr. Merrick came in with Lee's list of questions in his hand. His meeting with Lee was brief. He told him there was nothing more he could do for him. He was not going to get well, and in a day or so he would discharge him from the hospital.

Initially, I was enraged by the doctor's callousness. However, after I calmed down I realized that lying would have been pointless. Still, I think a word or two of encouragement would not have been amiss.

Dr. Merrick dealt with Lee's questions about the actual death process in the same professional, no-nonsense way. The carbon dioxide would build up in his brain until he would finally fall asleep and not wake up. In the meantime, when Lee wanted him to, he would order what he called a "hospice mix." It was a mixture of morphine and vistaril, and it should ease the pain.

I listened, stony-faced, afraid to move or think lest I splinter into a thousand pieces.

Just before midnight, Lee whispered, "Mom, are you asleep?"

"No, I'm just lying here thinking. Can I get you something?"

"No. It's just that I've been thinking—not that I expect to die soon—but maybe now would be a good time to talk about it. The nearer the time comes, the harder it's going to be for us to talk about what happens—you know—afterward."

Quietly, with no tears or faltering, he told me that he'd like his brothers and sisters to give the prayers and talks at his services. He had just begun enumerating a few things he wanted them to have when a coughing spell left him drained. The attack over, he leaned against his pillows, exhausted, eyes closed. I sat quietly beside him on his bed, rubbing his arms and hands, needing to touch him.

Monday, May 27, 1991:

Dr. Merrick started Lee on the morphine mix this morning. Lee is pleased that it eases his pain and makes breathing easier without making him drowsy. Actually, I had hoped it would help him sleep, for he rarely dozes off. When he does, he moans with each breath.

Tuesday, May 28, 1991:

At three o'clock this morning, Lee was fighting to breathe, and once more the nurse called in a respiratory therapist. What in the world am I to do when I get him home, and there are no professionals standing by? The nurses and therapists are doing their best to help me learn to care for him, but I'm sick with worry that in a crisis I will fail him.

Because I'm involved around the clock in Lee's care now, I've slept only a few minutes at a time since I started staying nights at the hospital four days ago. My fatigue must have been evident, because at noon today Kay and the nurse insisted I go home for a few hours' sleep.

I had barely closed my eyes when our oxygen supplier delivered an 800-pound liquid oxygen tank. It was too large to go through the door, so the delivery man placed it outside Lee's bedroom and ran a hose through a partially opened window. He thought that would work fine. Unfortunately, the controls are on the tank, which means we have to run out and around the house to adjust the flow! When I pointed that out, he gave me a blank stare, shrugged his shoulders like it was no big deal, and left. I'm too exhausted to deal with that now. I'll leave it for Kay to handle.

The children on our block watched the delivery of the huge tank with inquisitive eyes, and I had visions of one of them giving the valves a whirl. Rounding them up, I took them to where the tank stood, then explained its purpose and how important it was not to play near it. One of the smaller boys stuck out his chest and said importantly, "Don't you worry, Mrs. Belnap. If anyone tries to get near it, they'll have to go through me first!"

When I returned to the hospital, I was surprised to hear Lee laughing when I opened his door. He hadn't laughed aloud for a long time. He motioned me in. "Actually, it was quite fun having a broken nose, once it quit hurting," he was telling the inhalation therapist bending over him. "When you're nine, getting hurt playing sports is pretty neat. It not only earns you the respect of your teammates, but all the girls cluck over you." Grinning, he introduced me to Mr. Coby. "It was his son, Greg, who threw the bat that broke my nose in the fourth grade," he explained.

Mr. Coby acknowledged the introduction with a smile. "You have a gracious son, Mrs. Belnap. He claims the accident was all his fault, that he shouldn't have been in front of the backstop."

With a flash of his old humor, Lee shot back, "I don't know about the gracious part, but I'm no dummy. I'm not about to blame someone whose dad is regulating my oxygen!"

Mr. Coby and Lee had spent over an hour experimenting with various types of oxygen masks, and had found that his sats (oxygen saturations) were consistently higher when he wore the "rebreathable" type. The mask was a cumbersome thing. It had an air reservoir that hung down to his abdomen, and wearing it made speaking even more difficult. But that couldn't be helped. In his case, it was more oxygen-efficient.

Tonight, Lee was tired but cheerful as he told me about his afternoon. Reed was in Boise and had come to see him; and Janet Howard, the hair dresser who cuts his hair when he's in Boise, had given him a haircut. "She's a fun person, always good for a laugh," he chuckled. "She hadn't seen me since I've lost weight; and when she came in, she looked me up and down and said, 'Isn't it a shame I've so much body, and you've so little? I ought to squeeze you until we're both a perfect ten.'" Visualizing the scene, he chuckled again and said, "What a fun way to gain and lose weight. Too bad it doesn't work that way."

Wednesday, May 29, 1991:

Lee is in his own bed tonight; and, after the pandemonium in his hospital room this morning, he's relishing the quiet. Because he was scheduled to be discharged immediately following his noon I.V., nurses, dieticians, therapists, diabetic specialists, and, who knows who else converged on his room, all talking at once, each intent on giving me last-minute instructions.

Adding to the confusion, the I.V. had inexplicably stopped dripping. Two nurses, plus Jan Pincock, my nurse friend who will serve as a backup should I need her, were noisily discussing possible solutions. I was torn between needing to keep an eye on what they were doing should the blasted thing stop at home, and the equally urgent need to concentrate on the nurse's demonstration of how to measure Lee's glucose.

All the while, the inhalation therapist, anxious to get to his next patient, hovered at my elbow, wanting to assure himself that I understood the importance of properly disinfecting the equipment.

Suddenly, Lee's voice cut through the din. "That's it," he exclaimed, shooing at them with his hands, "the lessons are over. Anything else she needs to know, I'll teach her at home." Heads jerked around as startled eyes riveted on the exasperated patient glaring at them from his bed. This was the first impatience they'd seen in him during the two weeks they'd nursed him.

An older nurse, waiting to check me out on medications, was the first to recover her wits. With an apologetic nod in Lee's direction, she said, "Except for those working on the I.V. pump, let's all clear out and give him some quiet."

Lee closed his eyes gratefully. Using their softest voices, Jan and the two nurses turned their attention back to the balky pump. Finally the problem was solved, although no one could tell me exactly how, or even what the problem had been. I'm trying not to worry about what I'll do if it refuses to work in the middle of the night with no one to help me!

Along with Lee, we brought home four large garbage bags filled with tubing, masks, needles, glucose bags, and everything else the nurses thought we might need. I was still sorting out the mess when the home care nurse came at 6:00 p.m. to watch me give him his I.V. She will come two or three times a week to check Lee's vital signs and make a report to Dr. Merrick.

It's 1:30 a.m. now, and everything seems to be going smoothly. I had no problems helping Lee with the feeding tube and giving him his insulin shot. At 11:00 I nebulized and clapped him, and at midnight started his I.V. again. It takes two hours to drip through, so at this point, it still has another half an hour to go. I'll reset the alarm then, because an hour later he'll need enzymes to help him digest the Pulmocare. Three hours later, another day will begin. Makes for a long day, but he's home and so far no glitches! With the Lord's help, I may be able to do this yet.

Thursday, May 30, 1991:

Toward morning, Lee was struggling so hard to breathe that I panicked and called my nurse friend, Jan. She suggested turning his oxygen up to nine or ten liters for half an hour to see if that would help. It did.

While this was going on, Lee, either hallucinating or talking in his sleep, shouted, "All right! Our offense is on the move!" While I was panicking, he was enjoying a Borah football game! I didn't know whether to laugh or cry, so I did both.

The day before we brought Lee home from the hospital, I made out a detailed care schedule. I'm glad I did, because as I get more tired, it becomes harder to remember all the little details—and there are hundreds of those. Lee's care goes around the clock, and I find my days and nights are getting mixed up. Every four hours there are hour-long inhalation treatments, and every six hours there are two-hour I.V.'s—the kind I have to watch closely. Sandwiched in between are enteral feedings, glucose checks, insulin shots, medications, disinfecting of equipment, and Lee's personal needs. Once in every twenty-four hours, there is a three-hour period with nothing scheduled!

All of this doesn't leave much time for such mundane things as cooking, washing clothes, eating, or sleeping. Kay, of course, helps with everything he can, especially the drainages and keeping up the house. Even so, we'd never make it were it not for our children and kind friends who keep a steady stream of dinners coming to the house. How will I ever repay them?

Friday, May 31, 1991:

Carol Wood called from Salt Lake. Charlie had to go back into surgery to fix a leak and is now fighting a bad infection. He is once again on the lung donor list. When I told Lee, he sighed wearily and shook his head, not commenting. Actually, what was there to say? Later, I went into the bathroom and had myself a cry. I cry often now, especially at night. Curled up in the chair at the foot of his bed, I weep silently, not wanting Lee to know, ashamed of my weakness in the face of his great courage and uncomplaining fortitude.

Once I said to him, "It's all right, you know, to cry."

He merely shook his head and answered, "The time for tears is past."

My only contact with Dr. Merrick is my weekly telephone call. Every Monday I dial his number, praying that he will suggest something, anything. He listens, but gives no answers. I know there is nothing more he can do, but still I feel abandoned, and, I admit, unreasonably angry. Why doesn't he come up with something?

Monday, June 3, 1991:

Carol Wood called at noon and said that Charlie died last Saturday. When I told Lee, he simply said, "I had so hoped that he would make it."

Friday, June 7, 1991:

The children living out of Boise come as many weekends as they can to see Lee and sit with him. This weekend, Steve and Kristy and Stan are here. During the week, Mary, Roger, and Irene often take turns spending the late evening hours with him while I snatch a few hours of rest, returning to their homes at midnight when I take over to do his meds. They offer to do more, but there is really not anything more they can do. They, along with solicitous friends, bring in food which they hope will tempt Lee's appetite; but he's too ill and short of breath to eat. At most, he swallows a few spoons of soup or a bit of watermelon before pushing my hand away. "I'll eat it later when I'm breathing easier," he promises, but he never does.

He rarely escapes into sleep, and when he does, it is only to doze, sitting hunched forward, either cross-legged on the bed or teetering on the edge, feet dangling over the side. He can't stand the elastic strap of the mask around his head. Instead, he holds the mask hour after weary hour in his hand, his arm trembling with fatigue. I often sit beside him, silently holding it for him. And always there is the terrible coughing and thick, dark globs of mucus, streaked with blood. When I dump it out of the disposable cup into the toilet, it sinks to the bottom like a heavy brown stool. How does he manage to breathe at all? Yet he goes on, never whimpering, never complaining.

Often, his eyes are dull, and he sits on his bed, head down, mask in hand, jerking with fatigue. But there are also good times when his color improves and his eyes are clear. We live for those hours. When they come, he makes the most of them, answering the letters and cards that flow in daily, returning a few phone calls to friends, and sometimes watching a favorite TV show or listening to a tape. During those times, my heart leaps and I think, "He's turning the corner. He's going to make it!"

I know he's thinking the same thing, and we grin at each other.

Sunday, June 9, 1991:

This morning Lee fell into the most peaceful sleep he has had since he came home. I was tiptoeing out of his room when he sat bolt upright and asked, "Did you read me my bedtime story?" When I assured him that I had, he replied, "We should be on Z then." I don't know what he was dreaming, but whatever it was, it was a pleasant dream for he smiled and fell asleep again. When he awakened a few hours later, he felt strong enough for me to give him a sponge bath and wash his hair.

A few hours later, Dr. Venning came to see him. Because of his bad back it's an effort for him to get around, and Lee was deeply touched by his visit. When he left, he gripped Lee's thin shoulder tightly. Was I the only one who noticed that he didn't add, "You're going to be all right, boy"?

Wednesday, June 12, 1991:

Dr. Merrick discontinued the bactrim after the noon I.V. Lee stays about the same. Most of the time he's alert, but there are short periods of time when he finds it difficult to think clearly. He hates those times, afraid he may be losing control. A few days ago he had me decrease his morphine, hoping that would help. It didn't make any difference, and today when he was struggling, he asked me to resume the full dosage.

I can't tell if his down periods are caused by the "mix" or by a buildup of carbon dioxide. Dr. Merrick and the home care nurses are vague. Apparently they can't tell without testing his blood gases, and they aren't inclined to do that. If I had an oximeter, I could measure his sats myself. I asked for a prescription to rent one, but the doctor feels it wouldn't be wise, that watching his sats fall and not being able to prevent it would drive me crazy. Perhaps it would; but I'd rather go crazy knowing what's happening than go crazy not knowing. I feel so terribly alone. Everyone has given up except for Lee and me.

Wednesday, June 19, 1991:

For a wonderful moment last night I was a child again, back in my old bedroom on the farm, snuggled under one of my mother's colorful patchwork quilts. I fancied I heard the murmur of Mother's and Dad's voices in the kitchen, the opening and closing of the oven on our old Monarch wood range, and the smell of biscuits baking. Through the window came the slapping sound of water tumbling over rapids in the only swift part of the big canal that wound through our farm. I scrunched down and pulled the quilt more closely around my chin.

Lee moaned, and the dream shattered. For the briefest of moments, I tried to summon it back, yearning to be a child again. However, the dream, like my childhood, was gone. My mother's old patchwork quilt was only a tied imitation; and the sound of the rapids was the water bubbling in the humidifier on the oxygen tank.

Sunday, June 23, 1991:

I seldom leave the house, but this morning I slipped over to hear our grandson, Tyler, give his farewell talk before he leaves on his mission to Uruguay next week. Jan Pincock, my nurse friend, cared for Lee. Jan is a tall, slender blonde, mother of five, possessor of a cheerful smile and a big heart.

I was nervous leaving Lee, but I needn't have worried. When we arrived home, there was Jan sitting spoon-fashion behind Lee on the bed, her long Sunday dress hiked up to her knees, a nylon-clad leg on each side of his thin buttocks, giving him his drainage. She was clapping his back with such enthusiasm that his body bounced with each clap. Lee was grinning broadly, relishing the sight they must make.

The Lord continues to bless us with the love of good friends. This time it was Jan, cheerfully rendering service minutes before she was to conduct a Relief Society meeting as second counselor.

Monday, June 24, 1991:

Usually Lee rallies for the home care nurse's visit, but today he was lethargic. Again, I asked if it was carbon dioxide building up or the morphine mix. She didn't know.

By afternoon, he was feeling better; and after Kay and I had given him a sponge bath and shampooed his hair, he surprised us by asking us to help him into the bathroom. Supporting himself against the sink, he shaved himself. This is only the third time he has been strong enough to walk to the bathroom since he came home from the hospital. Dare I hope that he is beginning to turn the corner and getting better?

Tuesday, June 25, 1991:

After Lee felt so well yesterday, I wasn't prepared for his abrupt shortness of breath this morning. Afraid that a lung was collapsing, I asked the home care nurse to come and listen to his lungs. She listened, but she didn't know. It could be that chunks of hardened mucus were working their way upward and interfering with his breathing; or it could be that more of the smaller airways were collapsing and shutting his breathing down. She would report it to the doctor. Neither she nor the doctor called back.

Wednesday, June 26, 1991:

Shortly before noon, Lee's Salt Lake doctor friends, Grant Burch and Steve Braddock, phoned and said they were at that very moment jumping in their car and driving to Boise to check Lee out for themselves.

The doctors were large, vigorous men; and when they bounded down the stairs into Lee's room and enveloped his fragile body in their arms, it was as if their very presence breathed new life and vitality into our home. They stayed for two or more hours, laughing uproariously at Lee's quips and regaling him with hospital tales of their own. Occasionally, they called me into the room and included me in their banter. When they left, they promised to come back tomorrow.

Thursday, June 27, 1991:

True to their word, Dr. Burch and Dr. Braddock came back at noon, bringing with them a set of headphones "so you won't drive your mother wild with your choice of music." Lee had me pull his photograph albums down from the shelf; and, with a doctor on each side of him, they huddled together on the bed, poring over the pictures, reminiscing and laughing, happily sharing memories the photographs evoked.

Then it was time for a goodbye hug, followed by a quick retreat before Lee could see the glint of tears in their eyes.

Saturday, June 29, 1991:

Lee had another bad night. He sat on the edge of his bed hour after hour, his feet resting on a stool, his eyes fixed on the luminous dial of the clock on his night stand. Once he dozed, and his fingers relaxed their hold on the mask and it fell to the floor. I picked it up and gently slid the elastic over his ears. Slipping his legs onto the bed, I eased him against the mountain of pillows at his back. For a few minutes he relaxed there, but all too soon the coughing and choking began. He doubled forward, and sleep did not come to him again.

Once I asked him what he was thinking. He said that he was reliving fun times he'd had with family and friends. His reply reminded me of a statement he'd made in a taped interview with Robin Johnson of the University of Washington Medical Center. Mr. Johnson was making a study of young adults with terminal diseases and had asked Lee what the secret was to getting through the hard times, especially those in the dark of night when he was alone and fighting to breathe. Lee had answered, "You have to find strength within yourself. You have to dig down deep and see what you're made of. It helps to have good memories to draw from. I can see how people give up if they don't have anything to draw from."

Mr. Johnson then asked him where he thought he got his strength, and Lee answered, "I think I got it from the way I was raised. I have many happy memories."

Now it's night again, and he sits on the edge of his bed, holding the oxygen mask to his face, patiently enduring still another long night. Again, I wonder what he's thinking. Is he wishing that just once more he could walk among the flowers in the backyard and pat the trunk of the old cherry tree that he used to climb? Does he long to go to church and greet old friends, poke his head into the gym where he used to play basketball, and maybe even walk across the parking lot to the softball field and relive a few triumphant moments there? Or would he settle for simply walking up the stairs that he used to fly up so effortlessly and looking down at the lawn where he and his brothers played touch football on a summer's evening and built snow forts and pelted each other with snowballs on wintry afternoons?

Perhaps those are only my wishes for him. Perhaps he has moved beyond such things now.

Sunday, June 30, 1991:

For the past ten days, Lee has been writing a letter or two a day to his friends and enclosing his picture. This morning he asked if I would finish them for him. He would tell me what to say if I'd type them and address the envelopes. The letters were brief and tailored to each individual. In them, he expressed his appreciation for his or her friendship. The only tipoff that this would be his last letter came at the end when he said, "Have a good life." I doubted if many would catch the subtle difference of being wished "a good life" rather than "a good day."

Extremely tired, he requested that he have no visitors except for those bringing him the sacrament. When they came, he shook the hand of each one and thanked them for their dedication.

Tonight for the first time, he had difficulty inserting the feeding tube into his stomach. When he finally got it down, he said, "You need to learn how to do this without my help. I may not be able to do it much longer." Then he told me that he loved me.

Monday, July 1, 1991:

During the night last night, Lee said he felt strange. Bright lights were dancing in his head. My breath caught in my throat. In a few minutes, however, he said, "I feel okay now, but I wish I could sleep. I'm very tired."

Gently I asked, "Do you want Heavenly Father to release you, Lee? Do you want to go home?"

He shook his head. "I want to stay with my family," he answered.

He was silent for so long that I thought he might have dozed off, but suddenly he whispered, "When do you think it'll be?"

"I don't know," I answered softly, "but I don't think it will be until you tell Heavenly Father you're ready."

He nodded his head and didn't answer.

This morning I wondered if Lee remembered our conversation in the night. If so, he chose not to mention it.

My personal prayers for Lee have changed. Now I simply ask that he go soon and peacefully with the dignity he so treasures intact.

Dr. Merrick said to discontinue Lee's feedings when he can no longer insert the tube by himself. I can't do that. It may be contradictory to pray for his suffering to end and then turn around and help him with the feedings that are keeping him alive; but as long as he chooses to fight for life, I'll continue to fight with him. We've been a team too many years for me to let him down now. I hope the Lord understands. I'm certain that He does.

Tuesday, July 2, 1991:

Lee was largely unresponsive until this afternoon. Then he became clear-eyed and alert. He asked if I had finished typing the last of the letters to his friends. I gave them to him, and he signed his name. He indicated he felt well enough for a sponge bath and shampoo, and afterward he tried to run the electric razor over his face a few times. Kay offered to shave him, but he shook his head. He still tries to do everything he can for himself.

Tonight, with my help, he guided the feeding tube through his nose into his stomach. He continues to fight for life, but he is dying and my heart is dying with him.

Wednesday, July 3, 1991:

Lee passed away at six o'clock this afternoon in his father's and my arms.

Wednesday, July 10, 1991:

It has been a week today since Lee passed away. There are no words to describe my sorrow. People tell me that the pain will someday be less, but I know it will never completely pass. The empty place in my heart will remain forever.

Roger sat with Lee the last night of his life. As he had done for weeks, Lee sat on the edge of his bed, hunched over, elbows resting on his knees, one hand holding the oxygen mask in place. Suddenly, he tried to stand, and his knees buckled. Roger caught him and lowered him to the floor, but not before he knocked the pitcher of water and medications off the nightstand. Kay came running from the other room; the three of us helped him back into bed, and Roger and I kept watch together the remainder of the night. Lee dozed fitfully. At 2:00 a.m., he was struggling to breathe, and I gave him a treatment.

He finally fell asleep propped up against his pillows, and when he awakened four hours later, he was alert and asked, "Did something bad happen during the night?"

"Nothing bad happened," I answered. "You slipped when you stood up and knocked a few things off your table. Roger caught you. Nothing bad happened."

He shook his head ruefully. "I don't remember falling. I just remember a loud noise and some confusion. My brain is going right down the toilet. I hate that."

"Your brain is okay," I assured him. "If it were really 'going down the toilet,' you wouldn't be worried. You were half asleep when you fell, and we all forget things that happen when we're sleepy. You're still very much in control."

All day he struggled. I prayed that he would sink into a coma, but he didn't. I knew of his concern for his father and me, and at one point I whispered, "Lee, it's all right if you let go now. Dad and I will be fine. If you want to go, it's okay."

He didn't answer. We held him in our arms all afternoon, telling him we loved him and how grateful we were to be his mother and father. Then, while the clock over the fireplace in the family room struck six, he died. His earthly mission was finished; he had gone home to his Heavenly Father.

Kay and I knelt beside his bed, his hands in ours, and tearfully gave thanks to our Lord for the blessing of being this gallant lad's parents. Then, rising from my knees, I gently smoothed his hair and sponged his dear face, yearning to hear him say just one more time, "Not to worry, Mom, I'm okay."

The words didn't come. They didn't need to, really, for now he's more than just "okay." Cystic fibrosis may have claimed his ravaged body, but his spirit never faltered. He lives on triumphantly, with all eternity before him. And someday, when our mission is completed, we shall hold him in our arms again.

About the Author

Karma Smith Belnap was born and raised in Idaho. She graduated from the University of Idaho with high honors, and she and her husband, Kay, have raised four sons and three daughters.

Now retired, Karma serves as a temple worker and is the visiting teaching coordinator in her Boise, Idaho ward. She has written a number of articles for local and national publications, including *Good Housekeeping* and the *Idaho Statesman*, and has lectured widely on the subject of cystic fibrosis.

One of the founders of the Idaho Cystic Fibrosis Chapter, she was instrumental in getting cystic fibrosis covered by the Crippled Children Services of Idaho and establishing a C/F clinic in the Nampa/Boise area. Karma enjoys writing, reading, family history research, and walking.